GUIDELINES

VOL 34 / PART 3
September–December 2018

Edited by **David Spriggs**

GW00689751

The Bible Reading Fellowship
15 The Chambers, Vineyard
Abingdon OX14 3FE
brf.org.uk

The Bible Reading Fellowship (BRF) is a Registered Charity (233280)

ISBN 978 0 85746 604 4

This edition © The Bible Reading Fellowship 2018
Cover image © Erikona/iStock

Distributed in Australia by:
MediaCom Education Inc., PO Box 610, Unley, SA 5061
Tel: 1 800 811 311 | dmin@mediacom.org.au

Distributed in New Zealand by:
Scripture Union Wholesale, PO Box 760, Wellington
Tel: 04 385 0421 | uwholesale@clear.net.nz

Acknowledgements
Scripture quotations taken from The Holy Bible, New International Version (Anglicised edition) copyright © 1979, 1984, 2011 by Biblica. Used by permission of Hodder & Stoughton Publishers, a Hachette UK company. All rights reserved. 'NIV' is a registered trademark of Biblica. UK trademark number 1448790.

Scripture quotations from The New Revised Standard Version of the Bible, Anglicised edition, copyright © 1989, 1995 by the Division of Christian Education of the National Council of the Churches of Christ in the United States of America. Used by permission. All rights reserved.

Scripture quotations taken from the Holy Bible, English Standard Version, published by HarperCollins Publishers, © 2001 Crossway Bibles, a division of Good News Publishers. Used by permission. All rights reserved.

Printed by Gutenberg Press, Tarxien, Malta

Suggestions for using *Guidelines*

Set aside a regular time and place, if possible, when and where you can read and pray undisturbed. Before you begin, take time to be still and, if you find it helpful, use the BRF Prayer on page 6.

In *Guidelines*, the introductory section provides context for the passages or themes to be studied, while the units of comment can be used daily, weekly, or whatever best fits your timetable. You will need a Bible (more than one if you want to compare different translations) as Bible passages are not included. At the end of each week is a 'Guidelines' section, offering further thoughts about, or practical application of, what you have been studying.

Occasionally, you may read something in *Guidelines* that you find particularly challenging, even uncomfortable. This is inevitable in a series of notes which draws on a wide spectrum of contributors, and doesn't believe in ducking difficult issues. Indeed, we believe that *Guidelines* readers much prefer thought-provoking material to a bland diet that only confirms what they already think.

If you do disagree with a contributor, you may find it helpful to go through these three steps. First, think about why you feel uncomfortable. Perhaps this is an idea that is new to you, or you are not happy about the way something has been expressed. Or there may be something more substantial – you may feel that the writer is guilty of sweeping generalisation, factual error, or theological or ethical misjudgment. Second, pray that God would use this disagreement to teach you more about his word and about yourself. Third, think about what you will do as a result of the disagreement. You might resolve to find out more about the issue, or write to the contributor or the editors of *Guidelines*.

To send feedback, please email **enquiries@brf.org.uk**, phone **+44 (0)1865 319700** or write to the address shown opposite.

Writers in this issue

Paul Bradbury is a pioneer minister based in Poole. As well as planting churches locally, he is involved in pioneer ministry across the south of England. His publications include *Stepping into Grace* (BRF, 2016).

Jeremy Duff is Principal of St Padarn's Institute, a centre for ministry training in Wales. His book *The Elements of New Testament Greek* (2005) is Cambridge University Press's bestselling religion title. He has also written *Peter's Preaching* for BRF (2015).

Miriam Hinksman (née Bier) is a visiting lecturer in Old Testament and research fellow at London School of Theology. She teaches and preaches regularly at her church in Canterbury.

Michael Parsons is a Commissioning Editor for The Bible Reading Fellowship and an Associate Research Fellow at Spurgeon's College, London. He has written several books including *Praying the Bible with Luther* (BRF, 2017).

Steve Motyer loves the quest for understanding – and the Bible is central to this quest. His life as a carer helps with this, as does 30 years of teaching New Testament and Counselling at London School of Theology.

Fiona Gregson is an ordained Anglican whose UK ministry has been mainly in inner-city, multicultural parishes. She has also lived and worked in several African countries.

Paul Hedley Jones is Lecturer in Old Testament and Homiletics in Australia. His teaching and writing seek to integrate theological interpretation of Old Testament texts with issues in spiritual formation.

Kate Bruce is Deputy Warden at Cranmer Hall, Durham, where she teaches preaching at BA and MA level. She did her PhD on preaching and imagination and has written a number of books and articles on this area.

David Spriggs provides consultancy services for Bible Society, but his main role is as a Baptist minister. He is a part-time minister with the Friar Lane and Braunstone Baptist Church, Leicester.

Steve Walton is a researcher and teacher of the New Testament. An Anglican priest, he has served in student and parish ministry. Steve has published a number of books, and is presently working on a commentary on Acts.

Andrew Lincoln is Emeritus Professor of New Testament at the University of Gloucestershire. His publications include substantial commentaries on Ephesians, Colossians and the Gospel of John.

David Spriggs writes...

'Who do you say that I am?' This question is put by Jesus to his disciples and is considered by Steve Motyer as he brings us to the conclusion of his studies on Mark 1—8. It is a question that as disciples we are always facing, and as ministers of the gospel we constantly need to refresh our understanding. We do this by re-engaging with the scriptures, which are our source of insight. Advent and Christmas provide us with a great opportunity to do this.

There are several weeks within these notes which help us achieve this. There is Andrew Lincoln's examination of the flourishing or abundant life which Jesus came to bring us. This offers us an amazing insight into John's Gospel and the incarnation. Along with this, there is the introduction to Luke's Gospel by Steve Walton, looking at the Advent chapters, and my attempt to provide a more in-depth context for appreciating the nuances of the birth of Jesus by considering other 'special births' within the scriptures.

One of the new authors for *Guidelines* is Paul Bradbury, who has published a book with BRF on vocation (*Stepping into Grace*, 2016 – available to order on p. 151). As he seeks to elucidate the relationship between vocation and ambition, we are taken into some of the depths of Christ's own ministry, helping us understand what it is to be 'the Christ'.

Our faith is incarnational, so Fiona Gregson considers how the early church was an incarnational community – in the way that they shared their possessions with one another. Michael Parsons, who in a previous issue introduced us to Luther's insights on prayer, now uses Calvin's understanding of prayer to further sharpen an appropriate Christian spirituality.

Jesus made it very clear to his disciples that being 'the Christ' inevitably involved suffering. The Old Testament provides a rich context for grappling with this paradox that Peter and most Christians since have also struggled with. Kate Bruce's contribution on Lamentations is truly helpful here.

Paul Hedley Jones explores how the prophets share in God's passion for redemption: 'Israel's prophets are precursors to Jesus, whose prophetic ministry brings about the fulfilment of God's passion to dwell on earth.'

Miriam Hinksman and Jeremy Duff both tackle challenging material. Miriam engages seriously with the text and challenges of Nahum and Obadiah. From her research into the book of Lamentations, she is well-placed to help us appreciate the distress which the other nations had brought to Israel when they invaded with arrogant and merciless brutality. Jeremy shares with us his deep appreciation of the biblical material surrounding gender issues. These contributions are vital for us if we are to be Christians committed to the Bible but aware of the challenges this can bring us.

5

The BRF Prayer

Almighty God,
you have taught us that your word is a lamp for our feet
and a light for our path. Help us, and all who prayerfully
read your word, to deepen our fellowship with you
and with each other through your love.
And in so doing may we come to know you more fully,
love you more truly, and follow more faithfully
in the steps of your son Jesus Christ, who lives and reigns
with you and the Holy Spirit, one God for evermore.
Amen

A vocational journey

Paul Bradbury

Vocation is under threat. The very concept of vocation has less and less value in a world where results, targets and the bottom line so often determine the agenda of our workplaces. I speak with too many people who have a deeply held sense of vocation but are thinking of leaving their jobs, because they do not have space or time to give expression to what they feel called to do.

Yet vocation is at the heart of what it means to be human. Beginning with Abraham and throughout the story of the people of God, we see that we are people responding to a call, drawn onwards by the voice of God on a journey of discovery and change. And it is not just a call to do this or that, but a call to grow into the fullest expression of who we are. Vocation is as much about being as it is doing. Our call is not only to do great things for God, but to be that which only we can be, and be that as fully as we can.

The story of Jonah, that ancient and mysterious tale of shipwrecks, whales and curious vines, has so often been reduced to a series of events. But really the book is as much about process – the process of transformation that takes place in Jonah as these events unfold. It is a story about Jonah's vocation as a prophet, while his career as a professional royal adviser is dismantled by a new call of God.

In the next two weeks, we will journey with Jonah, exploring as we go various issues around Christian vocation. There will be a few detours from the text of Jonah but the thread of this extraordinary story will be our main guide.

Unless otherwise stated, quotations are from the New International Version (Anglicised).

1 Ambition

The first word of the book of the prophet Jonah is a clue to the reader that this is no ordinary prophetic book. It is a word lost from some translations, including the NIV, but it is there in, for example, the NRSV: 'Now the word of the Lord came to Jonah.' That little word 'now' causes a complete divergence from the usual form. It tells us that this book is something rather different, because what we receive in some of our English translations as 'now' might well be translated as 'once upon a time.' Hence *The Message* translates this verse: 'One day long ago, God's Word came to Jonah.' We are being told a story. It is a story not so much about what Jonah says, or even what he does, but about what happens to him and how he responds.

Jonah is indeed a prophet. A little background research reveals that he was a prophet in the court of Jeroboam II during his reign over the northern kingdom of Israel. In 2 Kings 14:25, we are told that Jeroboam 'restored the boundaries of Israel from Lebo Hamath to the Dead Sea, in accordance with the word of the Lord, the God of Israel, spoken through his servant Jonah son of Amittai'. Jonah was perhaps a kind of divine adviser to the king's military ambitions. And, by all accounts, he was a rather good one and it may have served him rather well. He has perhaps built a rather comfortable career from speaking into the royal court. But all that is about to change.

Into this setting comes a new call from God: a new expression of Jonah's vocation and an invitation into a new context. He is asked to go and speak to the people of Nineveh – the capital of Assyria and the seat of power of Israel's greatest threat. By all accounts, this is a harsh and cruel regime. This is a vocation that, by the nature of its extraordinary challenge, puts everything about Jonah's call and career under threat. So he runs the other way.

Often, we make a distinction between vocation and ambition, as though vocation were somehow a holy thing and ambition its unholy opposite. But in Jonah we see a gift ambitiously expressed in one context being called into another. In this new context, everything is threatened, even life itself, while (as we shall see) vocation is enhanced. Ambition is not, then, a dirty word. We are called to express our gifts to the utmost. However, God is just as concerned with who we can become as what we can achieve.

2 Ambition in creation

Genesis 1:27—2:25

We detour from the story of Jonah for a couple of days in order to explore the relationship between ambition and vocation. To understand this relationship more deeply, we need to start at the beginning. The two creation stories offer two different perspectives on the role and place of humanity in creation.

The first narrative contains God's charge to humanity to 'fill the earth and subdue it. Rule over the fish in the sea and the birds in the sky and over every living creature that moves on the ground' (1:28). The emphasis of this account is on an active engagement in the stuff of creation. It is an invitation to work with the resources of creation, an invitation that is at the heart of the great achievements and innovations of humanity – and yet, also, some of its greatest abuses.

The second narrative, however, seems to focus more on relationship. Humankind is created and invited to engage in a relationship of care and harmony with creation (2:15). Adam's cry is for relationship with his fellow humans: for community in a lonely world. The invitation is to serve others in the cause of harmony and balance.

Neither of these roles is more moral or more desirable than the other; they are both part of how we are created. But they do live in apparent contradiction to one another. We are driven to create, to subdue, to use our intellect and ingenuity in the use of the materials we find around us in creation. We often call this ambition. However, we are also created to serve, to surrender, to relate, to offer something of that same self in sacrifice to the wider good, the broader community. Perhaps the word for this is vocation.

Vocation, then, is not a more moral alternative to ambition. Rather, vocation is the expression of ambition through the lens of sacrifice and service, through the prism of self-giving. We do not have to dump ambition at the threshold between one and the other; rather, ambition begins to take on a more mature form, still benefiting from the drive of the charge to subdue and create, but transformed and redeemed by a deeper call to offer one's gifts and talents in the service of others.

3 Jesus and ambition

Philippians 2:1–11

The relationship between ambition and vocation we explored yesterday is exemplified in the person of Jesus. This journey is a paradoxical one whereby the offering to God of our drive and ambition in the service of others creates space for the maturing of our gifts into a vocation. This is the way of Christ, the paradox of life laid down, life lost to discover life regained. This journey is expressed perfectly in the early church hymn of Philippians 2.

Jesus models the vocational journey. The awesome creativity and ingenuity of our ambition can tempt us towards 'equality with God' (v. 6). Jesus chooses to let go of that equality and models a life of service and sacrifice. He is confronting precisely the contradiction in our nature that the two creation accounts point to. He chooses servanthood and he accepts the humility of suffering and death, because to be fully human is to offer our very nature, with all its gifts and God-givenness, to others. Now the descendent journey is transformed into one of exaltation as he is lifted once again 'to the highest place' (v. 9) and given the position of ultimate honour where all humanity will come to acknowledge that he is Lord (vv. 10–11).

The journey from ambition to vocation begins with letting go. There is a distinct change of direction, a definite change of gear, when we begin to walk in vocation rather than ambition. Ambition is largely self-driven. We are motivated by something within us, something we struggle perhaps to articulate. It feels like something we must do, something that feels at first exciting and all-consuming. We are the ones pushing and urging ourselves on to achieve better and greater things.

The second part of the journey is different. The energy for the journey comes from somewhere else: from outside ourselves. We choose to lose ourselves, lay down our agendas and our goals, and listen to a different voice. We respond to the voice of God calling, even when it will call us beyond ourselves. This call draws on the material which has been driving us on so far, our natural gifts, talents and desires. Our true vocation is not something disconnected or different from our ambition. Rather, it is an ennobling, a transformation of our created qualities in all their raw material. If we let him, God will take these up and into his desires and his ambitions.

4 Flight

Back to the story of Jonah, in which his call to preach to the Ninevites is also a call to lay down his ambitious self and discover a deeper expression of his vocation. We do not let comfort and equilibrium go without a fight, however. And Jonah's call upward is met with a journey of descent down to the coast at Joppa (v. 3), on to a boat bound for Tarshish and 'down into the inner part of the ship' (v. 5, ESV) where he 'lay down and fell into a deep sleep' (v. 5).

Jonah's flight in the opposite direction is a desperate attempt to avoid God but, more fundamentally, it is an attempt to avoid the deep personal implications of the call God has made on his life. His choice of a ship to Tarshish is no accident. Tarshish was the land on the edge of the world, a land of myth and promise far, far away, laced with all the delicious uncertainties of the unknown, without the pressing responsibilities of the here and now. We all have a Tarshish – that place we dream of going to when it gets too much: stacking shelves in Tesco; retiring early; the next job that will surely be free of all that irks us in this one.

Anna Synletica, one of the mothers of the early desert monastic movement, gave this advice: 'If you are living in a monastery, do not go to another place. It will do you a great deal of harm.' This wisdom flew in the face of the constant temptation among many to avoid facing the challenges that their vocation was forcing them to face, and to find somewhere else less challenging. The advice grew, eventually, into the Benedictine vow of stability that advocated a commitment to staying.

In our mobile world of infinite opportunity, it is all too easy to run away. Our egos will scream at us to flee when something deeply precious within us, that we won't give up without a fight, is threatened by the call of God. Yet God, in his insistent wisdom, is calling us upward and onward, inviting us through challenges that often seem beyond us, to discover new depths to the possibilities of our vocation. Sometimes this may well look like moving on, doing a new thing. But often it means staying, resisting the urge to run away, and allowing God to change us in the midst of where we already are.

5 Learning to fall

While Jonah has been doing all he can to run away from God and his vocation, a storm has been brewing. This storm is not by chance; it is the providence of God (v. 4): the first in this story of a series of interventions in the natural world by God that are invitations for Jonah to grow, change and be transformed.

None of us welcome storms. We endure storms. Our theology of storms may well be that God is in our storms – an anchor in the storm – helping us get through it. But is God a provider of storms? Well, here he is, and this episode might well invite us to recognise our own experiences of storms for what they often are: opportunities for personal and spiritual growth.

For it is in the midst of this storm that a new journey begins for Jonah. It is the captain of the ship who demands that Jonah 'get up' and 'call out to [his] God' (v. 6, ESV). The irony of this would not have been lost on the original readers of the story, for this invitation is a deliberate reference to God's call on Jonah to 'Arise, go…' (v. 2, ESV) – only this time it is a pagan sailor making the invitation!

Stripped of the comfort and familiarity of political and religious life in Israel, with the storm raging around him and the container of his last attempt at self-determination beginning to sink beneath him, Jonah is invited to make a choice. Under interrogation from the sailors, he makes his confession: 'I am a Hebrew' (v. 9). Is this a sincere confession? I believe so: these are the words of a man who realises he now has nowhere else to go except in the direction of the God he reluctantly believes in. These words are the first tentative step towards not just confessional belief but relationship with a God who calls and provides.

And it took a storm to do it. Julian of Norwich once said, 'First there is the fall, then we recover from the fall. Both are the mercy of God!' Our experiences of storms, disaster, failure and falling are not aberrations to the work of God's mercy and grace. So often they are the necessary context in which his grace can be fully expressed, for they do what nothing else can do to bring us to our senses and step into the reality of what we say we believe.

6 Embracing the darkness

Jonah 2

Some have argued that the psalm of Jonah chapter 2 is a later insertion, it being so different in style from the rest of the book. But perhaps the story shifts from prose to poetry for a reason: to slow us down. This is the very heart of the story, the hinge point, the place where we arrive at the crux of the matter. This moment demands our attention. And, like Jonah, if we are to step back from our busyness and self-importance long enough to allow God to meet us, we need to slow down and be deeply attentive.

The work of theologians such as Claus Westermann and Walter Brueggemann has helped identify categories of psalms. Some psalms express thanks and praise to God. Others express protest and lament. Others, sometimes called 'psalms of reorientation', express wonder, surprise and awe at an intervention of God that has established a new state of well-being, peace and prosperity. The psalm of chapter 2, as Jonah descends into the darkness, the stench and the near-certain death of the digestive tract of a whale, ought, you might think, to elicit a psalm of lament. But no, this psalm, most of the language of which is drawn phrase by phrase from the psalms of Jonah's worshipping tradition, is in the form of a psalm of reorientation.

So it is in the darkness, the danger and the near-death experience of the whale that Jonah finds his voice of faith. At the rock-bottom moment in the story, having reached the 'roots of the mountains' (v. 6), the journey turns; there is revelation, a new insight, a new commitment. 'But you, Lord my God, brought my life up from the pit,' says Jonah (v. 6b) – and it is indeed Jonah, for these lines are no quotation; they are new, the genuine utterance of our diffident prophet. He has found his voice and, perhaps with it, a new confidence in his vocation.

Again, as with the storm of the previous chapter, it is negative experience that brings Jonah to this moment of epiphany. Darkness, so frequently shunned in our world of artificial lights and bright distraction, is the context for spiritual growth and discovery. Darkness, be it real or metaphorical, is an experience rich with potential for the presence of God and the transforming power of God. Darkness slows us, disarms us, makes us vulnerable and impotent – just the kind of effect needed to bring us to our senses and bring us to God.

Guidelines

Frederick Buechner wrote that 'vocation is the place where our deep gladness meets with the world's deep need'. The church has often implied that 'vain ambition' needs to be ignored and rejected in order to pursue a vocation. However, the story of Jonah, chiming with the creation narratives, suggests that our ambition is very much part of the material for the shaping of our vocation. The dynamic journey between one and the other is exemplified by the person of Jesus. As you reflect on this story, how do you respond? Are you ambitious? What are you ambitious for? How might your ambition relate to your own journey of vocation?

Jonah's flight was in response to a call he could not face. Tarshish becomes a metaphor for all the places we sometimes want to run to when the call on our lives seems beyond us. Do we have a Tarshish, real or imaginary? When we are tempted to go there, what effect does it have on our ministry? In what ways might God be at work in us as we grapple with the challenges before us?

For Jonah, a storm and the dark recesses of a great whale brought about a radical repentance and change of direction. How do you respond to the experience of storms in your life? What about darkness? Are they experiences to be ignored, resisted? Do we tend to soldier on regardless? What if God might be speaking to you? What if the difficulties and uncertainties you face are part of God's way of shaping who you are?

Perhaps spend some time reflecting on this and offering your response to God in prayer.

1 Limited abilities

Jonah 3

Reaching chapter 3, you could conclude that a simple story of call, disobedience, rebuke and restoration has been completed. The call to 'arise' and 'go to Nineveh, that great city…' is repeated (v. 2, ESV. This time Jonah responds, 'according to the word of the Lord' (v. 3, ESV).

Yet this is a far more nuanced tale than that. This book, written most likely after the exile, as Israel wrestled with the humiliating reality of being a minority in a pagan land, undermines the classic trope of the prophet-as-hero. As Jonah enters Nineveh, fresh from his humiliation at sea, we are told in detail the dimensions of this great city (v. 3). The implication appears to be that once more the anointed individual will bring about the miraculous intervention of God.

And yet there is no triumphalism here, even as God's words bring about transformation. Soon, Jonah will be described as an angry and confused mess in response to the repentance of the Ninevites. In disobedience or obedience, the limitations of Jonah's very ordinary humanity are exposed for the reader to reflect on.

Furthermore, no longer can we see other peoples and other lands through a lens of superiority. We must watch, listen, measure and learn, and be open to the work of God to surprise us and challenge us. We must journey through places with our eyes and ears open before we have the temerity to speak (v. 4).

In these verses, we see a foretaste of the incarnational mission of the early church – a movement birthed in the humility and servant-heartedness of Jesus, one that embraces the limitations of place and person rather than seeking some sort of heroic transcendence of them.

So, too, our own vocation as disciples, ministers and leaders of mission is earthed in the reality of who we are and where we are. The enormous expectations placed on leaders in the church, in an age of great anxiety, can undermine the gift of vocation. We collude with these expectations at our peril. The bodily and geographical context of our vocation is a holy thing. As Rowan Williams wrote: 'Where we are and who we are is the furnace where the Son of God walks.'

2 Losing our illusions

The repentance of the people of Nineveh is not a cause for celebration for Jonah. He is angry. And the source of his anger is made clear by the writer.

The Hebrew word *ra'* has been used to describe the evil of the Ninevites (3:8). The same word is then used when the Ninevites 'turned from their evil ways' (3:10) and again when referring to God's decision to withdraw the destruction (*ra'ah*) he had threatened. By contrast, all this was literally *ra'* to Jonah, and 'he became angry' (4:1). Jonah's anger is directly related to the merciful action of God. For Jonah, the *ra'* of the Ninevites should logically result in the *ra'ah* of God – when it doesn't, he is consumed by it himself.

Jonah spells it out clearly: he fled to Tarshish because he knew God to be 'gracious and compassionate… slow to anger and abounding in love, a God who relents from sending calamity' (4:2). He faces up to the truth that he could no longer embrace what he believed God to be. The grace of God was outstripping Jonah's ability to contain him. He ran away. Now faced with it again, he would rather die.

There is something slightly comical and melodramatic about Jonah's outburst. Yet it ought to eventually turn us to empathy and recognition. Jonah's world has been shattered. The plausible structure of his life and vocation has been shown to be an illusion. The flimsy booth he constructs at the edge of a foreign city, far from Israel, is a symbolic expression of what remains of Jonah's attempts at providing a coherent structure for his own life.

And yet it may well be the beginning of real life. The spiritual life that underpins all that we are and do grows through the loss of our illusions, and ultimately through the loss of our life. The foundation for the fullness of life that Jesus spoke about (John 10:10) is the one created by the loss of all the false structures we have created for ourselves. 'Whoever loses their life for my sake will find it,' says Jesus (Matthew 10:39). True vocation begins when we have laid down any pretence of control or understanding and offered who we are to the God of infinite grace.

3 On the threshold of grace

Jonah 4; Romans 5:1–2

Throughout this whole journey, God has been holding out an invitation to Jonah: an invitation to live, truly live, in a universe beyond the illusions of his own sense of control, security and identity, and within a world resting on the truth that it is the God of grace who is in control, who provides ultimate security, who affirms who we are.

Sitting in his booth on the edge of Nineveh, Jonah seems to be on the threshold, a watershed, between one life and the next. The God of compassion and mercy invites Jonah to trust him beyond the limitations Jonah had placed on him. A new world beckons.

The exiles, bewildered and broken, working out how to rethink and re-form their faith in a hostile environment, began to embrace the mystery of the grace of God. God was no longer fixed by the definitions of the temple or lines of ethnic divisions, or by the ever-changing boundaries of the kingdom of Israel – he had broken out.

It was much the same for the early church, learning to grapple with a God who had broken out beyond the bounds of Jewish people. Grace knew no bounds. So Paul rejoiced in the book of Romans in this new experience of grace 'in which we now stand' (Romans 5:2). Yet this is not just a new expanded vision of grace, with new boundaries just some way further out. The meaning of the verse is much more profound than that. The sense of the phrase translated 'gained access' is one of being introduced, like a suitor to a king or a guest at a function. The implication is one of movement, of being invited into a new world, in which we can live and explore.

And this is the kind of vocation that Jonah is now invited into. Instead of a rather static vision of God and what it means to serve him, one in which God is perhaps invoked to bless our efforts, Jonah is invited into the dynamic realm in which he can participate in the unfurling of God's grace in the healing of all things. The door of Jonah's booth is like the wide and generous door of the kingdom of God; the threshold is an invitation to enter into the adventure of joining in with a God whose purpose is nothing less than the redemption of all creation.

4 Waiting on grace

Many have asked why Jonah fled to Tarshish. Here, towards the end of the story, we appear to have an answer: 'For I knew that you are a gracious God and merciful, slow to anger and abounding in steadfast love, and relenting from disaster' (v. 2, ESV). But what is it about this characteristic of God that caused Jonah to flee?

One argument is that Jonah anticipated the repentance of the Ninevites. Their response would be a personal humiliation for him, in contrast to the stubbornness of the Israelites who he has been ministering to for so long. He cannot bear to return to Israel with a story of God's mercy to the Ninevites and their response, for the effect this will have on his reputation as a prophet. He would rather die than do that (v. 3).

However, there is nothing to suggest that Jonah's message to Israel has been one of repentance. It seems to have been more a message of political and territorial renewal (2 Kings 14:25). We can see Jonah's explanation not as a vindication of his assumption of how God would act, but as a revelation of the *extent* of God's willingness to act as this God. The extension of God's grace to the people of Nineveh shatters Jonah's framework for his whole ministry and life. His life is finished; he cannot conceive of his vocation in the context of this boundless grace, this unpredictable, unfathomable, uncontrollable mercy and love.

We might also see in this picture – of a broken, defeated man of God, waiting at the edge of the city of Nineveh (v. 5) – a glimpse of a truer way to be ministers of God's grace. For the beginning of learning to live in the world of grace comes in ceasing to be at the centre of events; ceasing always to have to be part of the action; ceasing to exert our power or agenda; ceasing to use God for our own ends and allowing God to use us for his. Learning to live in the world of grace involves learning to wait, often at the edge of things, and above all else waiting patiently and being attentive to what God will do. This is not an easy place. It may well feel as alienating, useless and exposed a place as Jonah's booth must have felt to him. But it is the place we need to cultivate and maintain in order to inhabit this world of grace.

5 Middle-voice ministry

Jonah 4:10–11

The writer of the book of Jonah invited us to ask at the story's outset, 'What will happen to Jonah?' The writer now asks, 'And what will happen now that his illusion of control has disappeared?' How will Jonah and God's action relate to one another now?

There is an exchange of both words and action, a give and take of statement and question, action and counteraction, as Jonah wrestles with God. Jonah makes a shelter. God provides a vine. Jonah is happy about this. God provides a worm which withers the vine. Then God provides a dry, hot east wind to wither Jonah himself. Jonah vents his anger. God challenges Jonah's anger. Jonah asserts it all the more (4:5–9).

Whereas previously whole sections of the story have flowed from the actions or words of God or Jonah, now the narrative is like a final showdown, a physical and verbal contest of increasing intensity. We await the result. We expect closure. We read on for the take-home message, a final and satisfying resolution.

Except there isn't one. The whole story ends on another question, one designed to take the reader to a place of reflection once more. If God can be as concerned with unreliable vines, herds of cattle and ignorant Ninevites as with the people of Israel, then his grace and mercy are far more wild, unpredictable and mysterious than we had ever realised! You've seen what this revelation did to Jonah, suggests the narrator. Now, how are you going to respond?

Ministry for many of us navigates the dynamic between our action and that of God. We are not wholly passive in this ministry we are called to, but then we are also dependent on the action of God. All too easily, we can tip into activism. We find we have, to use John V. Taylor's powerful phrase, 'turned the divine initiative into a human enterprise'.

However, there is a middle way or, if you like, a 'middle voice'. In this 'middle-voice ministry', we are neither active nor passive; rather, we are a subject that participates in the action that another has initiated. I believe this final question of the book of Jonah invites us, as it invites Jonah, into that kind of ministry and vocation – one where we choose to participate in the unfolding action and grace of God's initiative.

6 The contemplative life

Our journey with Jonah is coming to an end. Jonah's vocation has been challenged and radically shaped by his call to Nineveh. The book's first audience may well have heard it as they struggled to adjust to the calamity of exile. For them, this story asked probing questions about their vocation as the people of God. What did it mean to be God's people in a pagan culture without the comforts and stability of state, temple, land, religious freedom and identity? Who were they without all these externalities? Were they still the people of God? Could they be?

The writer of the book of Jonah does not answer any of these questions, but instead invites his/her readers to imagine a new expression of their vocation in the light of this story. It is an invitation to a larger space, a wider vision of grace – one in which God's activity is not constrained and in which they are encouraged to participate.

This vision is a foretaste of Jesus' vision of the kingdom of God articulated in the many parables he used to illustrate it. The agrarian parables in particular describe a kingdom that is powerful, mysterious, hidden and persistent, one in which we are invited to work, but one in which not all the work is ours.

In today's reading, the kingdom grows and develops whether the farmer 'sleeps or gets up' (v. 27a). The kingdom is a mystery we partner with (v. 27b). Working in the kingdom is a vocation of grace, where, yes, there are periods of hard work, but there are also periods of extended rest when the deep organic process of the kingdom continues 'all by itself' (v. 28).

This is a liberating vision! There is rest as well as work written into the fabric of the kingdom of God. Where does it take us? Not to passivity – leaving the kingdom to do its work by itself – but rather to contemplation. Contemplation is that attitude of life and of spirit which is always listening, always watching, in an expectant, unhurried way, in order that we might lend our gifts and enterprise to the kingdom project. We listen in order to participate, not dominate. We constantly seek God, who is already at work in the field, the community, the individual. We trust that by God's grace we get to participate in a process that will bring a natural harvest (v. 29), not through our endeavour and enterprise, but through our attentive engagement.

Guidelines

The final two chapters of Jonah initially appear to offer conclusion and then offer anything but. They invite us to consider our own response to the story of Jonah. This is a book of questions, not answers. The story raises questions – about the fate of Jonah, the fate of the Ninevites – but in exploring them, it turns the questioning on us.

Would you respond any differently from Jonah? In what ways have you limited how and when and to whom God can act? Do you trust that God can best minister through you despite your limitations? Who is the main agent in your ministry? You? God? Have you turned the agency of the Spirit into a human enterprise?

The final chapter acts as an extended invitation to the reader of the book to a landscape of active grace which we are encouraged to explore and participate in. We are invited to find a 'middle voice', whereby we are constantly waiting and listening in order to participate in the ongoing growth of the kingdom of God. This contemplative attitude is therefore critical to the ministry of the kingdom – one which often proves challenging in a busy world and an anxious and, at times, demanding church.

As we come to the end of this journey with Jonah exploring vocation, perhaps reflect on how your vocation might become more responsive to the invitations of God's Holy Spirit. How can you cultivate an attitude of contemplation within the reality of your life and ministry?

Gender in the Bible

Jeremy Duff

Gender matters. Most people see it as fundamental to their identity but find the current discussion of it bewildering. For much of the last 50 years, a standard definition held: *sex* was biologically determined (in our chromosomes), but *gender* was a cultural construct. Thus whether you *were* a man or woman was fixed; what it *meant* to be a man or woman was a product of human traditions, understandings and practices. This is different again from questions of sexual morals – for example the sexual revolution of the 1960s and 70s questioned understandings of when and with whom men and women should have sex, not what 'man' or 'woman' meant. Similarly, campaigns for same-sex marriage didn't question ideas of gender, but simply argued that people of the same gender should be able to marry. But understandings of gender were also being challenged. In the UK, the 1970s began with the Equal Pay Act and finished with the first female Prime Minister. The following decades saw much effort to remove barriers to allow women of talent and skill to perform the same role as equally skilled men. What it means to be a woman or man shouldn't include expectations of what job you could do.

The last decades have seen concepts of gender continue to evolve. What does it mean for a woman to lead 'as a woman', not squeezing herself into a role shaped by male approaches and models? What is masculinity when male-dominated manual labour diminishes in importance in the economy, and young women out-perform young men in education? At the same time, though, a new strand of discussion has emerged, which questions not just gender but sex itself. The concepts of 'intersex', 'non-binary' and 'transsexual' challenge the idea that our biology simply determines whether we are men or women in the first place.

The Christian churches have found it hard to respond with clarity to these changes. Tensions have emerged between approaches which emphasise sexual morality and family life, and those which emphasise justice and equality. Much discussion within the churches has also been inward-looking – about the gender and sexuality of ministers. This is unfortunate, for in wider society there is much unease and searching for helpful understandings of gender, family and sexuality. It would be good if Christians were able to be 'salt and light', with wisdom to offer on the issue of gender.

These notes do not intend to 'answer' these questions, nor directly engage with the issues of the moment. Rather, we will look at twelve important passages in the Bible which relate to gender and carefully attend to what they say, trusting that, by doing so, we will find ourselves better equipped to act and speak with God's wisdom on this issue; indeed, that we might be 'transformed by the renewing of [our] minds' (Romans 12:2).

Quotations are expressed in my own translation; the notes can be used with any modern English Bible.

1 God's Spirit for all

Acts 2:17–21

Why start here, rather than with creation in Genesis, stories of Jesus, or passages in the epistles which tease out gender relations? These notes begin here at Pentecost partly because of the first four words 'In the last days' (v. 17). Theologically, this is where we are living – 'in the last days'. Jesus has won the victory (Colossians 2:15); we wait for Jesus' return (1 Thessalonians 1:10); we have the Spirit as a deposit of what will come (2 Corinthians 1:22; 5:5); we have a task to complete (Acts 1:6–8). Humanity has entered a new epoch, in which the 'old way' of 'law' no longer rules (Luke 16:16; Galatians 3:23–25). Our search is for wisdom about gender for the world we live in today – for these 'last days'.

Moreover, gender features significantly in this prophecy from Joel, quoted by Peter at the beginning of this Pentecost speech. That 'all flesh' can or will receive God's Spirit might be the main point (vv. 17, 21; compare Luke 3:6), but it is developed as 'sons and daughters', 'young men and old men', 'slaves, both men and women' (vv. 17–18). 'All flesh' carries a broad meaning – old and young, Gentile and Jew, slave and free, from all nations (1:8; 2:9–11, 39) – but some real emphasis is put on gender: men and women.

The emphasis was needed. Greek thinking was dominated by Aristotle who said, 'the male is by nature superior, and the female inferior; and the one rules, and the other is ruled' (*Politics*, 1254b2–10). Jewish thinking can be seen in the words of the first-century writer Josephus: 'The law says that a woman is worse than a man in all things' (*Against Apion*, 2:200). If, in these 'last days', God is coming to and speaking through women as to men ('prophesy', vv. 17–18), this is a shocking truth which would need to be proclaimed. We saw this starting in Jesus' own ministry, where women were the key financial backers of Jesus' ministry (Luke 8:1–3), and the ones entrusted with the message of the resurrection (Luke 24:1–12). Mary was the first to meet the risen Jesus (John 20:11–18).

Much of Acts depicts the breaking of boundaries with Gentiles coming into the faith (e.g. Acts 11:18; 15:5–6). Here at Pentecost, the boundaries of the way in which gender was understood also seem to have been broken.

2 A woman gives birth to God

Luke 1:26–55

The incarnation – God becoming flesh – is perhaps the most distinctive doctrine in Christianity. God does not just enter into our world by his Spirit, or appear in human form, but God *becomes* body, sharing flesh and blood, like us in every respect (Hebrews 2:14, 17).

Jesus was male – Mary gave birth to a son (v. 31). Intriguingly, Christian theology has never made much of this maleness. It has always been acknowledged, but seen as part of the 'scandal of particularity' – God being born in a particular place, at a particular time, in a particular way – but theologically what is important is God becoming human, flesh and entering our world (John 1:14–18), not that he took on a particular gender, race or hair colour.

At the same time, it is Mary, a woman, who is declared to be 'favoured by God' (vv. 28, 30) and proclaimed as 'blessed' for all time (v. 48), and by whose willing sacrificial obedience God's plan for salvation is enacted (v. 38). A male Jesus was dependent on a female Mary. Understandably, in many churches Mary has become the archetypal female disciple, but with a variety of implications – from understandings dominated by giving birth and nurturing children (as Mary clearly did) to those emphasising women's role as crucial agents in God's plans through the exercise of great faith (as Mary clearly was).

Elsewhere in Luke's Gospel, we find that male and female are carefully balanced. Scholars talk of Luke's 'gender pairs' – rarely do we find a story about a man without a corresponding one about a woman: Simeon and Anna (Luke 2:25–38); the centurion's servant and the widow's son (Luke 7:1–16); the searching shepherd and seeking woman (Luke 15:1–10). Stories about humans have to be stories about men and women. At the same time, as we saw at the first Pentecost, male and female are not the only division within humanity. In her song, Mary does not emphasise her femaleness, but her humility, fear of God, lack of power and poverty. Yes, a woman has this crucial role in God's plan, but she herself interprets it as honouring her in her poverty and humility, rather than through the lens of gender.

3 Creation

Genesis 1:26–28; 2:18–24

Our passages today extract the parts involving gender from the creation stories, which seem to have different approaches. In Genesis 1, humanity from the first moment is created male and female (1:27), while Genesis 2 depicts woman's creation arising because something was lacking in the man. This is not unusual – what is said second focuses on a particular of what has just been said to explain it more fully. So Genesis 1 gives the overall picture – that God created humanity as male and female. But if we ask, 'Why?', Genesis 2 provides an answer. One gender alone is lacking, and that lack cannot be made up from the rest of creation (2:19–20). Male and female are intricately and intimately linked ('bone of my bone', 2:23). Men and women are not from different planets; they are not different species. They might be different, but they are closer to each other than to anything else in creation.

Three further things emerge from these passages. First, it is male and female together that are said to be in God's image and likeness, and to whom the duty of guardianship over the rest of creation is given (1:26–28). The image and commission are for humanity as a whole; indeed, one gender on its own would be lacking.

Second, we need to avoid interpreting Genesis 2:18 and 24 in a crude way. No human is a half-person, desperately needing their 'other half' to complete them. Such use of language is deeply distorting of our understanding of humanity, and damaging to those who are single. This passage's wisdom that 'alone is not good' and that one gender by itself is lacking does contribute to our understanding of marriage (v. 24) but has far broader and richer implications.

Third, these passages seem to suggest that at creation – in God's intention – humanity exists in two sexes; sex is an 'either/or', even if gender is a more fluid human construct. This is challenging for the ideas of intersex or transsexual people. However, this passage gives no backing to any ideas of what it means to be a man or to be a woman. 'Not identifying as a man' may well mean not identifying with a culturally constructed, potentially damaging sense of what a man is that gains no support from this passage. Furthermore, central to Christian theology is the idea of 'the fall' – that life as experienced now is not as God intended it. Thus one could argue that God's intention might be that sex is a biologically fixed 'either/or', but that this doesn't match sex as experienced now, and so we have to seek godly ways of living in an imperfect world.

4 Describing God

Isaiah 66:10–16

Nobody has ever seen God (John 1:18). Jesus is the visible image of the *invisible* God (Colossians 1:15). God is beyond our understanding (Isaiah 55:8–9). As we think about gender, it is important to remember that when we use human language to describe God, we are doing a necessary but woefully lacking and imprecise task. When the Bible speaks of God as a lion (Isaiah 31:4) or an eagle (Deuteronomy 32:10–12), we have to be careful. This language tells us something true and meaningful about God, but there are many things about lions and eagles which are not true of God. The image (metaphor) was used in a particular context to communicate a particular aspect of God.

Much of the language used to communicate God uses metaphors from humanity, such as shepherd, king and father, and therefore gets tied up in human gender. This is itself an intriguing phenomenon – suggesting that God prefers to be described in personal terms, despite the problems of gender, rather than in impersonal terms (for example, the force, light, love). In some cases, we easily look past the gender. For example, even if shepherds tended to be male, when Ezekiel 34 speaks of God acting as a shepherd for his people, we readily think about shepherding not maleness. In other cases, though, the gender seems more intrinsic to the image – most obviously in Jesus teaching us to address God as 'our Father' (Matthew 6:9).

Our passage today illustrates this complexity of using human language to speak of the invisible God. First (vv. 10–11), the Jewish exiles, suffering hardship and a sense of abandonment, are encouraged with a beautiful description of Jerusalem as a mother with comforting, sustaining breasts overflowing with the sustenance and security which the troubled baby needs. Then (vv. 12–13) God says that he himself will comfort the people 'as a mother comforts her child'. The best way to communicate God's intention towards the people is through the use of the language of a mother. Then (vv. 14–16) it is explained that this will be God's nature towards his servants, but towards his foes the picture is of fire, sword and chariots. The best way to communicate God's intention towards these foes is through the use of the language (the metaphor) of a warrior and battle.

God is neither a mother nor a warrior but in these passages this language helps bridge the gap between us and the invisible God. We are reminded of the tightrope we walk. We need, and the Bible fully supports, metaphors of people (who inevitably have to be women or men) to describe God, but God is not male nor female. God isn't human. God is beyond us. God is God; but God wants to be known.

5 No longer male and female

Galatians 3:23–29

What does it mean that there is no longer male and female (v. 28)? How does this fit with what we have already seen and other parts of the scriptures? Paul is working within the same sense of time that we saw in Acts 2. A change has come ('until Christ came… but now', vv. 24–25). Before there was restriction ('imprisoned', v. 23), but now there is release. The 'male and female' clause is one part of a triplet alongside 'Jew and Greek' and 'slave and free'.

The rest of Paul's writings give us some clues as to what this might mean. When we think of 'slave and free', we find that Paul does not think that this distinction has actually disappeared; indeed, he gives particular instructions and advice to slaves about how to live given that they are slaves (e.g. Colossians 3:22–25). But within the Christian community, the distinction is subsumed under the recognition of the other as 'brother' (Philemon 16) and a missional imperative (1 Corinthians 9:19). Similarly regarding Jew and Gentile: the difference remains (Romans 3:1–2), but both now have an equal place in God's mercy (Romans 10:4).

Intriguingly, at two other places Paul gives a similar statement ('no longer Jew or Greek…'), but in both places omits 'male or female' (1 Corinthians 12:13; Colossians 3:11). Why? One explanation is that 'neither male nor female' can easily be taken to mean the fact that people are women and men is abolished. But as we have seen, Genesis 1 and 2 describe 'male' and 'female' as part of God's good creation. It is different from slave and free (a human creation) and Jew and Gentile (part of God's plan for the salvation which has now come; see Genesis 12:1–3). Our passages next week explore this more.

So it seems that this passage doesn't mean that there are literally no longer men and women, for that would be to contradict our daily experience and God's intention at creation, but that women and men have the same status and honour. Formerly that was not the case – women were seen as lesser, as is sadly still true in so many societies – but as we saw in Acts 2, the boundaries of the way in which gender is understood are now broken; in Christ, women are lifted up.

6 The fall

Genesis 3:14–19

This passage provides the missing piece of the jigsaw. As we noted in the notes on Acts 2, the dominant understanding in ancient Greek and ancient Jewish thought was that men were created to rule and women to be ruled. But our reading of Genesis 1 and 2 suggested something different: that men and women were created to share in ruling; that at creation there wasn't a power dynamic between them. This understanding was confirmed by our reading of Galatians 3. 'In Christ' we should manifest God's intention at creation – female and male are both heirs of God.

Sadly, as we look at human society, we see that the ancient Greek and Jewish description seems often to be accurate – women are ruled and dominated by men. But as we noted in our reading of Genesis 1 and 2, a core Christian belief is that our experience of the world now does not indicate God's intention. (Hence the ethical slogan, 'You can't deduce an *ought* from an *is*.')

This passage is clear. The effect of human sin (described in 3:1–13) is to bring distortion and hardship into God's creation. This is described in relation to the labour traditionally associated with both genders – the woman's labour in childbirth and the man's labour in the fields. Both are now full of toil and pain. But the distortion and pain also affect the relationship between the genders: the woman will desire her husband even though he will rule over her (v. 16).

Thus the notion of ruling or dominance, which so often has characterised understandings of gender, emerges as a feature of human sin. Our passage alerts us that this is what we will find in our world, and indeed what will arise within us, yet it is not God's intention or our calling in Christ. We use medicine and machinery to make childbirth and farming safer and easier (fighting against the effects of the fall); surely we should equally do what we can to counteract the impact of sin on the relationship between men and women.

Guidelines

If difference leads to domination and exploitation, it is tempting to try to remove difference. If Mary being honoured as a woman who gives birth to God is going to be distorted into the idea that a woman's role is to bear children, or that women who don't have children are 'lesser', it is tempting to marginalise this honouring of giving birth. If using language such as 'Father' for God is going to be distorted into the idea that God is more like a man than a woman, it is tempting to abandon all comparisons between God and humans, and talk of God as an impersonal force, or abstract ideal. If male and female is constantly twisted into dominance and power, it is tempting to try to sweep away the distinction between male and female completely.

But our calling is to resist those temptations: to honour Mary's role as Jesus' mother; to rejoice that human life can point to God; to seek to live out a way of male and female relating which is free from power and dominance, while rejoicing in the difference God created. And, indeed, to respond with great gentleness to those who struggle with the 'either/or' of two genders because we recognise that our own experience and understanding of gender may be far from God's intention.

What would it mean in our lives to turn away from the 'broad road' (Matthew 7:13–14) of rejecting difference, or of saying 'how things are is how they should be', and instead take the 'narrow road' of trying to live out an understanding of difference, and particularly of gender, in which power and dominance have no place?

1 Sex and marriage

1 Corinthians 7:1–7

In this week's readings, we move from the big picture regarding gender and look at some passages which work this out in particular contexts, beginning with this passage from 1 Corinthians. It's an intriguing letter. Can we identify any links between the host of problems Paul addresses?

Here, the Corinthians are saying that having sex is off the agenda ('It is well for a man not to touch a woman', v. 1), while elsewhere they seem to be engaging in too much (or the wrong kind of) sex (chapters 5—6). People seem to be abandoning in worship the traditional appearances of men and women (hair length/head coverings, 11:2–16), to be obsessed with 'speaking in tongues' (chapters 13—14), and to think that they have already arrived at the heavenly gates (4:8–13). One way of joining these dots is to see that the Corinthians thought they were now 'spiritual beings', 'like the angels', as demonstrated by the fact that they 'spoke in the tongues of angels' (13:1). But angels are beyond human gender, so when they joined in heavenly worship (praying and prophesying), they believed they should throw off the trappings of human gender; and since angels don't have sex, they believed they shouldn't either. For others, 'having arrived' and being spiritual beings meant what they did with their body didn't matter.

Thus (returning to our passage) some Corinthians believe that they are spiritual beings, beyond the distinctions of male and female which underpin sex. Paul gives a clear 'no'. Not only should 'each man have his own wife and each woman her own husband' (v. 2), but they should not 'deprive one another except perhaps by mutual agreement for a set time' (v. 5). Sex is not just permissible but, it seems, to be a frequent core element of marriage. The married believers in Jesus are not moving beyond being women and men.

More striking, though, is the reciprocity. Everyone in Paul's day would have expected him to say that the wife should give her husband his 'conjugal rights', and that the husband has authority over her body (vv. 3–4), but they would have been shocked by his assertion that precisely the same is true the other way around – the wife also has conjugal rights and has authority over her husband's body.

Paul gives us here a groundbreaking picture of equality within marriage. He resists the temptation to say that men and women are the same. Instead, he tackles head-on the problem of the fall. In marriage, difference comes together, but the power dynamic between men and women, caused by human sin, has no place among Jesus' disciples.

2 Single is better

1 Corinthians 7:6–9, 25–40

Many people experience Christian churches as being obsessed with families, meaning couples with children. Many single people report encountering the outlook that single people are okay under 30 (when they are 'on the way' to getting married – or even worse, 'on the way' to being proper adults) and okay when they are 'old people' (losing their positions as adults and now needing to be 'looked after'), but that it is married couples who are seen as the basic building blocks of the church.

Paul is having none of it. At the end of his stunning exposition of reciprocity within marriage, he adds, 'I wish that everyone was like me' (v. 7) – meaning single. The whole passage is fascinating, including his admission that, while this teaching is not explicitly 'a command of the Lord' (v. 25), he is confident it is God's will (v. 40). But for our thinking about gender, what matters most is that singleness is seen as at least as equally valid and honoured a state as being married.

In our reading of Genesis 2, we noted that the saying 'it is not good for man to be alone', and the idea that one gender on its own is lacking, need not only relate to marriage. Single people are not 'half-people' waiting for their 'other half'. That is important, but we might push it further. If gender difference hasn't been removed in Christ (just the sinful power dynamic) and singleness is honoured, then gender difference is not only important within the context of marriage or sex. Paul and Jesus were not lesser men because they were not part of a marriage unit with a 'woman'. Single people are fully gendered too.

The early church caused great scandal by saying that men and women did not need to marry but could lead significant, honoured lives (through the institution of monasticism), fully gendered, yet not sexually active. What would the modern equivalent of that be?

3 Keep your gender

1 Corinthians 11:4–16

This is one of those passages about which it's easy to scratch your head, thinking, 'I don't understand.' Most of us find it hard to agree that 'nature itself' teaches that a man shouldn't have long hair but a woman should (vv. 14–15), and don't know what to make of the language of shame (vv. 4–6). It seems so rooted to the culture in ancient Corinth that we aren't sure what value we draw from the passage. Nevertheless, if we avoid getting drawn into controversies and details, three important points regarding gender emerge.

First, we see Paul's careful undermining of any power dynamic within gender relations. He voices the standard view of the time – 'man was not made from woman but woman from man' (v. 8, drawing on Genesis 2:21–23) – but then points out that every man was born from a woman (v. 12). Thus 'in the Lord', neither gender is independent of the other (v. 11). There is a mutuality and reciprocity, but not sameness.

Second, there is the odd statement that 'a woman needs to have authority on her head because of the angels' (v. 10). There is nothing to suggest that this means she needs a sign of *someone else's* authority over her – that is just to insert into the text patriarchal ideas ('husband ruling', which Genesis 3:16 sees as the consequence of sin). Rather, her prophesying and praying in church would have been shocking in Paul's day – therefore she needs a sign that she has the authority to do it. 'Because of the angels'? Well, probably this means that 'the powers' will also be shocked. Women no longer being ruled – the consequence of sin being overturned in Christ – challenges and overturns the 'elemental spirits of the universe' with all of their rules (Colossians 2:8–23).

Third, all the business of length of hair, veils and 'reflected glory' may be deeply rooted in a culture we don't understand, but the overall point is very clear: both genders should pray and prophesy, but the men should do it 'like men' and the women 'like women'. The references to 'nature' and 'custom' (vv. 14, 16) seem to make clear that there is no divine command as to what being 'like men' and 'like women' should mean in practice. But it seems to be vital that, despite the attitudes of their day, the Corinthian women don't give in to the suggestion that to pray and prophesy they need to 'become like men'. Or, indeed, that both men and women need to give up their gender and become 'like the angels'.

4 Weaknesses and warnings

1 Timothy 2:8–15

This passage starts with an interesting gendered piece of advice: the men should avoid arguing and anger, and the women should avoid obsession with their looks (vv. 8–10). When I read this, I am torn. I am uneasy at the gendered advice; one of the values of my culture is that we treat people as individuals, not as members of a group. On the other hand, I find it hard to deny that Paul is on to something – we might all be better off if men argued less and women didn't worry so much about their appearance.

The final sentence takes some thought. It clearly can't mean that women are saved through giving birth to children, because Paul is very clear that we are saved through what Jesus has done on the cross, and we receive that by grace (Romans 5:6–11; Ephesians 2:1–10). And, of course, there are many women who don't give birth. The key is to see that the Greek literally says, 'She is saved through *the* childbearing.' This would be a normal Greek way of saying 'through giving birth', but it equally could be pointing to a particular childbearing. Which? That of Jesus. For Paul has just referred to the story of Adam and Eve (vv. 13–14) which could seem to imply that Eve was the doorway through which sin entered the world. So immediately Paul refers us to the fact that a woman was also the doorway through which salvation entered the world. Any negativity because of Eve is overturned because of Mary. Women have no particular burden to repent of; they just need to continue in faith, love and holiness (v. 15) – just as we all do. Once again, we see gender difference, but also a rejection of putting one gender down.

What then of verses 11 and 12? A difficulty here is that the word often translated 'have authority over [a man]' is unique in the whole of Greek language, so scholars find it hard to be sure what it means. It doesn't simply mean 'have a position of authority'; it has a sense of 'seize authority' or even 'manipulate authority'. This might connect with the Adam and Eve story, which was not about Eve being given a position of authority but her persuading Adam to do what she wanted. Paul asserts that women should be learners (disciples) in verse 11, but there is something he doesn't want, which he sees as linking with the Adam and Eve story. The answer, I suggest, is that some women were being deceived, copying the actions of Eve, taking authority which wasn't theirs and causing harm. They needed to stop. There is no reason to take this as meaning that all women are always going to copy this bad example. In the same way, the story of David and Bathsheba (2 Samuel 11) warns us about male use of power for sexual exploitation, but doesn't mean all men are destined to copy David. Nevertheless, our text makes clear that we need to take seriously such weaknesses and the harm they can cause.

5 Relationships in marriage

Ephesians 5:21–33

It's easy to say (with Paul) that gender difference is not removed in Christ, but sin's twisting of difference into exploitation should be rejected, but what does this mean in practice? Our sense of what it means to be a woman or a man has come from a culture full of ideas of power – 'the battle of the sexes'. It is hard to rethink that. Fortunately, though, in this passage Paul unpacks in some detail his understanding of relationships within marriage.

He starts with his shocking message: because of Christ 'be subject to one another' (v. 21) – shocking because, in his day, nobody would have thought a husband was in any way subject to his wife (compare the reciprocal rights and authority being encouraged in 1 Corinthians 7:3–4). Ancient Greek household codes only gave instructions to husbands, parents and masters; Paul's letter is shocking for addressing the wives, slaves and children as well, as if they are equally moral agents who can decide how to live.

So the big picture is the rejection of power dynamics and the assertion of mutuality between wife and husband. But Paul then goes on to unpack this differently for the two genders. The wife should be subject to the husband (v. 22) but the husband should give himself up (die) for the wife (v. 25). If you want to reduce this to the dubious question 'Who makes the final decisions?', this would mean the husband does but he always decides in favour of what his wife wants! Of course, male society has tended to twist this back to the sin-caused picture of Genesis 3:16 with men ruling, by pushing the 'subject to' and back-pedalling the 'give himself up [die] for'. But it would be a mistake to reject it all. There is something profound in the idea of marriage being between equal but very different people and, if you are married, it's worth pondering whether something good may come from a husband focusing on giving himself up for his wife and the wife focusing on being subject to her husband. Or, as Paul summarises it in verse 33, the husband giving love and the wife giving respect.

6 Heirs

Our final passage pulls back from the detail of particular relationships and situations to remind us of the broad theological framework. It has some close connections with Galatians 4:1–7, which immediately follows on from Galatians 3:23–29, which we studied earlier.

Something has fundamentally changed. In the new era, humans can now live in a different way. In Acts 2, boundaries were broken because God's Spirit was being poured out. So, we too now live in a different way because we are 'in the Spirit', indeed because 'the Spirit of God', that is 'the Spirit of Christ', is in us (v. 9). This transformation is as profound as the difference between death and life (v. 10). The transformation is not yet complete – we await the resurrection of our mortal bodies (v. 11). But we note that the transformation includes our bodies – our hope is not to become 'spirits' escaping the body. This fits with our reading of Genesis as depicting God's intention which he will re-establish once sin and its consequences are re-moved: they will have bodies, including being male and female, but they will be transformed. We see this in the appearance of Jesus after his resurrection, who still seemed to be male, and in Paul's discussion of the resurrection in 1 Corinthians 15:35–57, where he coins the phrase 'spiritual body' to catch this sense of transformation, but a body nonetheless.

Verse 14 makes clear that all of the followers of Jesus – all those on whom God's Spirit has come – are sons of God. Sons? Should we just blink and think 'sons and daughters'? No, because the passage goes on to discuss inheritance (v. 17; compare Galatians 3:29—4:17). In Paul's day, women did not inherit; only men did. So if Paul had written 'all those on whom God's Spirit has come are sons and daughters of God', his hearers would have taken this to mean, 'You men are heirs of God, co-heirs with Jesus; you women are valued, but not heirs.' The inequality, the consequence of sin with male rule, was written into the understanding of the very language Paul was using. So Paul calls the women followers of Jesus 'sons' because calling them 'sons' was the only way to ensure that they were not seen as second class compared with the men, and that Jesus was seen as their brother too.

Guidelines

Abstract theology is always easier than practical godly wisdom. In the first week, we saw that God is beyond gender, but that we were created to be male and female. Sin distorted that difference into a power dynamic – male ruling – but through Jesus, through the gift of God's Spirit, these (and other) boundaries can be broken. As Christians, we are called to live out that vision in which there is difference, particularly of gender, but in which power and dominance have no place.

In practice, we have seen that this is difficult. There is a constant tendency for one of two problems to emerge: either (a) the sinful distortion reasserts itself, and women's God-given equality is stolen; or (b) in reaction, people assert that gender difference doesn't exist, or is not God's intention, and the only way to avoid oppression is for us to be androgynous, not men and women, or indeed for women to ape men (think of the power-dressing women in jackets with large shoulder pads in the 1980s and female politicians taking testosterone to lower the pitch of their voices). Our readings have shown Paul trying to explain and work this out in practice, in his culture, resisting both the understandings of gender in his day and the temptation to throw away gender difference completely. It is a bit messy.

What about us? Can we work out in our own lives a practical godly wisdom for being a woman (or a man) which celebrates and finds real meaning in us being a man (or a woman), while also being wise about the dangers and temptations which come our way? If the battle of the sexes and abandoning the idea of gender are both wrong, what would 'right' look like in practice? What is your next step in thinking about, or living out, your gender? How might this benefit others?

Obadiah

Miriam Hinksman

Old enemies die hard. The book of Obadiah is an oracle against one of Israel's most enduring enemies, the nation of Edom (compare Jeremiah 49:7–22). South-east of Judah, Edom had a long history of enmity with Israel, traced back to twins Jacob and Esau struggling in the womb (see also Genesis 25; 27; 36; Numbers 20:14–21; 2 Samuel 8:13–14). According to biblical tradition, the Edomites are descended from Esau and the Israelites from Jacob: they are brother nations. But Edom has not behaved in the spirit of that brotherhood, and this, declares the Lord through Obadiah, will be their downfall.

The most likely historical setting for Obadiah is that of the destruction of Jerusalem by the Babylonians in 587BC (see 2 Kings 25). Biblical tradition holds that Edom stood aside, gloating; or even took advantage of Jerusalem, encroaching on their territory, when the Babylonians invaded.

Obadiah is short – a scant 21 verses – and so it is worth considering its position in the minor prophets to give some further context to the oracle. In the Hebrew Masoretic text and in English Bibles, Obadiah comes after Amos, and can be read as an expansion of Amos 9:12, envisaging a day when Israel will 'possess the remnant of Edom'. In the Septuagint (the ancient Greek version), however, it follows Joel, where judgement of Edom on the day of the Lord provides context (Joel 3:18–19). Either way, Obadiah is clear that Edom has not behaved as a brother ought, and that this situation is not to be tolerated. Yahweh will make things right: Israel will again possess their own land, as well as Edom's, and 'the kingdom shall be the Lord's' (v. 21).

There are two main parts to the book. Verses 1–14 and 15b pronounce judgement on Edom, while verses 15a and 16–21 announce the day of the Lord for 'all the nations' – a day that will spell disaster for Edom and restoration for Israel.

Unless otherwise stated, quotations are taken from the New Revised Standard Version.

1 I will bring you down

Obadiah 1–4

The superscription in verse 1 identifies the prophecy as 'the vision of Obadiah'. Very little is known about Obadiah the prophet. There are no identifying details within the text – no king named, no father, no hometown (compare, for example, Amos 1:1). Tradition identifies our Obadiah with Ahab's servant Obadiah, contemporary with Elijah in the ninth century BC (1 Kings 18:1–16). But Obadiah, meaning 'servant [or] worshipper of the Lord' is a fairly common name, occurring at least a dozen times in the Old Testament, so there is no real reason to think these two are one and the same.

The opening verses announce that judgement is coming to Edom. Such oracles against the nations are found throughout the prophetic books (see, for example, Amos 1—2 and Jeremiah 47—51). Obadiah is unusual, however, in that it is entirely addressed to a nation other than Israel or Judah (compare Nahum and Jonah, whose prophecies are addressed to Nineveh). While formally addressed to foreign nations, the oracles against the nations have the effect of reassuring Israel and Judah that God is sovereign and just, and will exercise judgement on all the nations accordingly.

The formulaic 'Thus says the Lord God' (v. 1) makes clear that these are God's words concerning Edom, not just Obadiah's, and emphasises the covenant name of Yahweh. Verse 1 describes a message being sent out to call the nations to rise up against Edom. The use of the plural 'we have heard' could be in reference to the divine council, conjuring the image of Yahweh consulting with courtiers as a king would do. Alternatively, it might indicate the prophet putting himself together with the people of Israel as the audience of this message about Edom.

Verses 2–4 are almost an object lesson of the proverb 'pride goes before a fall'. Edom is depicted as setting itself up in the heights. As well as being figurative language, this references the geographical reality of Edom – a mountainous and rocky land. The word for rock (v. 3) is the same as the word for Edom's capital city, Sela, which was situated on a plain in the mountains and as such was almost impenetrable. Like the eagles, Edom saw itself as lofty and out of reach (vv. 3–4).

Yahweh answers the Edomites' rhetorical question 'Who will bring me down to the ground?' with the definitive 'I will bring you down.' Edom's pride of heart has set it up for a fall. Its lofty dwelling place within the natural defences of the mountains has lulled it into a false sense of security.

2 Nothing left, all cut off

Obadiah 5–9

After the announcement of Yahweh's intention to bring Edom down, verses 5–9 go on to emphasise the totality of Edom's destruction. Verse 5 uses two images to demonstrate this complete end. First, there is the image of thieves arriving in the night, who 'steal only what they wanted'. Second, there is the image of grape gatherers, who, in keeping with Levitical law (Leviticus 19:9–10), leave some fruit behind for gleaners. The rhetorical thrust of the two images is that, while in both these cases there would be something left behind, in the case of Edom there will be *nothing* left behind – 'How you have been destroyed!' (v. 5).

The 'treasures' of verse 6 may refer to secret vaults or caves in the rocky terrain of Edom, which have been plundered and emptied. Even Edom's so-called friends and allies have turned against it (v. 7), which is ironic, given the way in which they themselves treated their supposed brother Jacob.

Verse 8 explicitly introduces the motif of the day of the Lord – the coming day of judgement when Yahweh's punishment will be meted out. In Obadiah, it is understood that this day is in the past for Israel and Judah (see v. 11), but in the future for Edom and the nations. Their turn to be judged will come, and things will be made right – scores will be settled for their part in exacting God's judgement on Israel and Judah in the first place. Although addressed to Edom, then, the oracle also operates as a message of 'comfort' for Judah – an assurance that God will make things right by doing to Edom what Edom did to them (compare v. 15). This is uncomfortable reading when set in relief against Jesus' message to love your enemies.

Verses 8 and 9 contribute to the emphasis of complete destruction for Edom – both Edom's wise ones and fighting men will be destroyed. In the words of Samuel Pagán, Edom's destruction will be 'conclusive and absolute' ('The Book of Obadiah' in *The New Interpreter's Bible Commentary*, Abingdon Press, 2015, p. 621).

3 You really shouldn't have

Now that it is clear that Edom is to be judged and destroyed, the reasons for this judgement are spelled out: 'For the slaughter and violence done to your brother Jacob' (v. 10). This is most likely referencing the part Edom played in Jerusalem's downfall in 587BC, with later tradition even suggesting it was the Edomites themselves who set fire to the temple. The name Jacob is used, rather than Judah or Jerusalem, to emphasise the brotherly relationship, and the term 'brother' also appears in verse 12.

The failure of Edom to act as an ally in keeping with the ancient bonds of brotherhood appears periodically in the exilic and post-exilic literature as a source of some bitterness to Judah (see, for example, Lamentations 4:21–22; Psalm 137:7). Rather than coming to his brother's aid when Jerusalem was invaded and looted by enemies, Edom stood aside and watched, and even worse, became 'like one of them' (v. 11).

Verses 12–14 consist of a series of negative commands, with a regular repeated reference to 'the day' of Judah's ruin. In the NRSV, the negative commands are translated 'You should not have', referring back to what Edom did and didn't do on the day of the Lord's judgement against Judah – that is, the 'day' the Babylonians invaded Jerusalem in 587BC. Edom is accused of standing aside and watching as Jerusalem was invaded (v. 11); gloating, rejoicing and boasting at their downfall (v. 12); entering the city and looting their goods (v. 13); and even cutting off any escapees to hand them over to their enemies (v. 14). Their transgressions thus progress from passively standing aside and simple Schadenfreude (vv. 11–12), to actively entering the city and aiding and abetting the enemies (vv. 13–14).

The message to Edom is clear: 'You shouldn't have done it.' The corresponding message to Judah is that their grievances against Edom have been upheld. As Edom is on the receiving end of God's judgement, his brother Jacob is vindicated.

4 As you have done, it shall be done to you

The day of historical judgement on Judah (vv. 12–14) gives way to the eschatological day of judgement for the nations. In analyses of the structure of Obadiah, commentators generally agree that verse 15b fits better as a finish to the first part of the book than 15a. Following on from the clear message to Edom that they 'should not have' done all the things listed in verses 11–14, the resulting 'As you have done, it shall be done to you' (v. 15b) makes perfect sense. The message for Edom is that their deeds have not gone unnoticed and that they will be repaid in kind for their actions against Judah.

Conversely, verse 15a is considered a better fit with the remainder of the book (vv. 16–21), which elaborates on the coming day of the Lord as it applies to all the nations: 'the day of the Lord is near against all the nations.'

Verse 15 is thus pivotal, marking a transition from attention on Edom to a more general judgement against the nations. The 'day' of the Lord that has figured so prominently in the first part of the oracle is emphasised again. This time, however, rather than a historical day of judgement upon Judah (associated with the Babylonian invasion of Jerusalem in 587BC), the 'day' of the Lord is envisaged as an eschatological day of judgement for the nations, and a day of vindication for Israel and Judah. The day of the Lord's judgement on Israel and Judah is past; but the crimes of the nations and their roles in enacting the Lord's judgement on Israel and Judah have yet to be punished.

Verse 16 elaborates on this theme of recompense for the nations, with the addressee changing from Edom in verses 1–14, to Israel and Judah in verse 16. As Israel and Judah have drunk the cup of God's wrath in Zion, so the nations will drink and be destroyed (compare Jeremiah 25:15–16, 27). The image of 'drinking' in Zion may also refer to the drunken celebrations of military victors, in which case the addressee here could still be Edom. As the addressee is not stated, it is difficult to determine which is meant, and it may be an intentional ambiguity, conjuring the historical image of ribald drunken soldiers profaning the holy hill, alongside the literary image of the cup of God's wrath poured out in judgement.

5 The Lord has spoken

Obadiah 17–18

If the temple mount was profaned by the Edomites in verse 16, now it is announced that it will once more be holy. The brotherly relationship is once again to the fore, with Edom referred to as the 'house of Esau' and the restoration of Jerusalem and Judah described in terms of the 'house of Jacob' taking back their possessions. The NRSV's translation that they 'shall take possession of those who dispossessed them' is an elaboration of the more straightforward translation, 'They shall possess their possessions.' This probably refers to the lands that have been taken by enemies coming back into their possession, as is elaborated in verses 19–20.

There is also a reference to the 'house of Joseph', in poetic parallel to the house of Jacob (v. 18), which could indicate the existence of a remnant of the northern kingdom of Israel coming together with the remnant of Judah in Jerusalem.

This theme of a 'remnant' on Mount Zion in Jerusalem (see also Isaiah 4:2–4; 7:3; 10:20–22) is contrasted with Edom's fate. Unlike the remnant of Judah, there will be 'no survivor of the house of Esau' (v. 18, but contrast Amos 9:12). Moreover, Israel and Judah will play a part in performing God's judgement on Edom, becoming the fire and flame that will burn up the house of Esau.

The closing formula 'The Lord has spoken' indicates the end of a unit, closing the oracle of judgement.

6 The kingdom shall be the Lord's

Obadiah 19–21

The Hebrew text of verses 19–20 is difficult, with a number of unresolved issues in identifying the referents of particular terms, resulting in differences in translation across different versions. For example, the NRSV specifies 'those of the Shephelah' taking hold of the land of the Philistines (v. 19). The NIV, however, translates this as 'people from the foothills' rather than identifying a particular region. In verse 20, the NRSV establishes the exiles in 'Halah' as possessing 'Phoenicia as far as Zarephath', while the NIV has 'the land as far as Zarephath' being possessed by the 'exiles who are in Canaan'.

The thrust of the verses, however, is quite clear: the exiles of Israel and Judah will return to the land and take possession of territory that has been occupied, extending their borders in all directions.

The area of the Negev (also 'Negeb') is mentioned both first and last in the delineation of territories that will be restored to Israel and Judah, book-ending all that comes between. This is perhaps significant given the tradition that Edom took advantage of Jerusalem's fall and exile to encroach upon this particular territory. All of the land specified, however, is to be restored to Israel and Judah, extending her borders to just about the same as those thought to be in place during the time of King David.

Verse 21 is considered by many commentators the key to the book of Obadiah, providing the principle that alleviates the vengeful sentiments of the previous verses somewhat. The land is to be restored to Israel and Judah, yes; but more than that, the kingdom will belong to the Lord. There is here an eschatological focus on the centrality of Yahweh's rule from Zion. There is a special role for the remnant of Israel, but the vision is that *Yahweh* will rule and reign from Zion. There is no mention that a human, Davidic king is envisaged when the exiles return to Zion to take up possession and governance of the land. The future is theocracy (compare Revelation 11:15).

Guidelines

It's hard to know quite how this small oracle against one of Israel's enemies might apply to us today, but there are some observations that can be made. The Edomites' misplaced trust in their supposedly secure situation in the mountains (vv. 3–4) might raise questions for us about in what or whom we put our trust. The outward appearance of physical strength, safety and security isn't enough to stand against the judgement of God 'on that day'.

To our ears, the punishment pronounced on Edom might sound overly harsh, even considering their blatant disregard for the bonds of brotherhood in a time of war. For Christians more familiar with Jesus' words of love for enemies and forgiveness for persecutors, and the injunction to 'do unto others as you would have them do unto you', this kind of tit-for-tat judgement makes for uncomfortable reading.

And yet the *lex talionis*, the principle that 'as you have done, so it shall be done to you', was enshrined in Levitical law, and theoretically had the effect of *limiting* revenge, rather than allowing wanton destruction in retaliation for perceived wrongs. In this light, the judgement pronounced on

Edom for his treatment of his brother Jacob was no more than he deserved. And in the context of Judah's devastation, hearing that their brother nation would get their comeuppance would surely have given some measure of vindication to the victims. Further, the principle of a final day of judgement on which all scores will be settled and all injustices made right is a theme that follows through into the New Testament (compare Matthew 25:31–46; Revelation 21).

What do you think? Is it a comfort to you to read that God will punish the enemies of the people of God? Hyunhye Junia Pokrifka-Joe suggests that:

Obadiah assures us that God will bring just retribution on the enemies of God's people, for vengeance belongs to the Lord (Deuteronomy 32:35; Romans 12:19). This should produce in women and men humility, forgiveness and compassion rather than hypocritical judgement, vindictiveness or triumphalism when our adversaries or abusers (within and outside the faith or family) undergo God's judgement or endure misfortune, lest we ourselves be judged by God.

'Obadiah', *The IVP Women's Bible Commentary* (Intervarsity Press, 2002), p. 457

Do you find this quote helpful? Why or why not?

When all is said and done, *God* will be the judge, and rule and reign.

FURTHER READING

Leslie Allen, *The Books of Joel, Obadiah, Jonah and Micah* (Eerdmans, 1976).
John Barton, *Joel and Obadiah* (Westminster John Knox, 2001).
Samuel Pagán, 'The Book of Obadiah', *The New Interpreter's Bible Commentary* vol. V (Abingdon Press, 2015), pp. 609–30.

John Calvin on prayer

Michael Parsons

John Calvin's thoughts on prayer are best discovered in his monumental work *Institutes of the Christian Religion*. Book 3, chapter 20 of the *Institutes* is long, but well worth the effort. When people say to me that they want 'to get into Calvin', this is the chapter I encourage them to read. It shows a man endowed with a sense of who God is in relation to humanity: there is undeserved grace and generosity on God's part and weakness and gratitude on ours. The chapter has a mature warmth and spiritual confidence. As we will see, it underlines the truth that all we need is in Jesus Christ.

Despite the fact that elsewhere the reformer writes concerning prayer, 'I lay down laws for no one' (*Letters*, 2.362), his chapter on prayer begins with four important and profound rules for praying; rules to govern the believer's 'true prayer'. It is a good place to start, for these will be at least implicit in the following notes, as you'll see.

The first rule is that we should approach God with a heartfelt sense of reverence, a realisation of who he has revealed himself to be, in acknowledgement of his sheer difference. Second, we should come to God with a genuine sense of our own weakness and need (including that of forgiveness) – a realisation of who we are before the sovereign and holy God. Third, we should address God with humility, surrendering all confidence in ourselves, being confident only in him. Fourth, we must come with a sure hope in the grace of God.

Three images pervade Calvin's writing on prayer. It is a conversation, he says. Coming to the Lord, Christians must adopt the person and disposition of a beggar. The third metaphor and the most dominant is that of a child drawing near to their father. And throughout the chapter is the insistence that Jesus Christ is central to our praying. These thoughts will shape the notes for the following week.

Quotations are from the New International Version (Anglicised).

1 The purposes of prayer

Psalm 86

Calvin states that the chief part of worship 'lies in the office of prayer'. His followers through the centuries since the Reformation seem to have prioritised the sermon; others of us the singing – but for Calvin it is prayer that lies at the heart of worship. The reason for this appears to be because it is in prayer that the relationship between the Lord and his people is most intimate, originating as it does in the very heart of the believer (see tomorrow's notes).

According to the reformer, there are five purposes of prayer:

- to approach God with every need
- to present him with all our supplications
- to encourage us to be humbly receptive of God's benefits, with gratitude
- to contemplate God's benevolence
- to confirm God's providence in our lives, instilling a spirit of delight or joy for his answers to our prayers.

It's worth, perhaps, pausing a moment and reflecting on each of these purposes in your own experience of prayer. How might these encourage you to pray more 'effectively'?

In writing Psalm 86, the psalmist illustrates these purposes quite clearly. But before we look at them, it's worth noticing that he acknowledges just who God is: he speaks of him as 'my God' (v. 2; see v. 4), affirming that there is no one like him among the gods (v. 8) and that all will one day worship him, bringing him glory (v. 9): 'you alone are God' (v. 10).

The psalmist evidently approaches God with all his needs; he calls upon him all day long (v. 2), asking for strength, mercy, teaching, godliness and deliverance. He is grateful for all of God's blessings towards him and receives them humbly (v. 1, 'for I am poor and needy'). He looks towards the Lord's goodness (vv. 1–4), and he appears to be assured of this on the basis of past benevolence. He calls upon God because he has answered him in the past (v. 7); he knows what God is like (vv. 15, 17).

And so, when facing enmity and danger (v. 14) from 'arrogant foes', the psalmist comes before his God whom he can trust, and who he knows from past experiences of grace will answer present supplication with faithful compassion.

2 Prayer as intimate conversation with God

There is no doubt that the psalmist in Psalm 95 expects worship to come from the heart – singing, joy, thanksgiving, bowing down, shouting! He speaks of God in exalted terms: he is 'the great King above all gods' (v. 3); he is 'our God' (v. 7), before whom everyone will bow. But there is a sense in the psalm that a conversation is happening – at least, that it might happen – and that those who hear should be cautious: 'Today, if only you would hear his voice, "Do not harden your hearts"' (vv. 7–8). Prayer is conversation.

The closest that Calvin gets to defining prayer is his claim that it is 'an emotion of the heart within, which is poured out and laid open before God, the searcher of hearts'. Prayer begins in the heart of the believer. God desires that we 'descend into our heart with our whole thought' and 'enter deeply within'. So prayer for Calvin is something that causes us to focus within, into the heart, because it is there that the Lord looks for 'a sincere and true affection'. His reasoning is straightforward: since we are God's temple, 'if we would call upon God in his holy temple, we must pray within ourselves'.

Prayer begins in us, but it doesn't remain there. For Calvin, prayer is a back-and-forward movement; ultimately, he describes it as our heart being 'lifted and carried beyond itself'. In this context, the reformer employs a telling image, which he picks up several times in his exposition of prayer. Indeed, his first rule (in his own words) is that 'we should be disposed in mind and heart as befits *those who enter conversation with God*'. Later, he speaks of God's generosity in admitting us into what he calls 'intimate conversation' with him.

The metaphor of conversation with God is useful, but neither the psalmist nor the reformer want us to get the wrong idea. God is God, after all. To him belongs glory and honour; it is proper that we enter into conversation with him humbly and with considerable thought and care.

Prayer is intimate conversation with God. Do we see it like that or are we too engrossed in a monologue to hear the divine voice?

3 A beggar seeking blessing

Luke 18:9–14; Jonah 2:1–9

The Bible is full of the idea that, as we approach God, we have nothing to offer. In Jesus' wonderful short parable of the Pharisee and the tax collector, for example, the second man recognises his own lack before God; he consciously humbles himself (Luke 18:14) and pleads and waits for generous mercy from the Lord. He comes as a beggar approaching God, mindful that he has nothing, but that God has all that he needs. Likewise, the prophet Jonah deliberately seeks God only when he feels his life ebbing away (Jonah 2:7). All he could do at that pivotal moment was to cry for salvation which comes from the Lord (v. 9) – like a beggar seeking grace!

We saw yesterday that Calvin sees prayer as a conversation. But who is the conversation between? One picture that resonates with biblical imagery is that of a beggar approaching a benefactor. This emphasises a sense of weakness and vulnerability in the supplicant and a sense of strength and capability in the God to whom we turn. The beggar approaches someone who is immersed in riches. The image appears explicitly only once in Calvin's long chapter on prayer, but is surely implicit elsewhere: 'It is… by the benefit of prayer that we reach those riches which are laid up for us'; and 'he will cause us to possess abundance in poverty.' Explicitly, it appears in the following:

It follows that only sincere worshippers of God pray aright and are heard. Let each one, therefore, as he prepares to pray be displeased with his own evil deeds, and (something that cannot happen without repentance) let him take the person and disposition of a beggar.

The image is a conventional one, of course – Calvin uses it elsewhere, as do most of the major reformers. But we notice that Calvin speaks of what appears to be a self-conscious decision: the believer has to '*take* the person and disposition of a beggar' before God. This, then, is the position of faith. It is an acknowledgement of our own poverty, together with recognition of the divine riches which are found only in Christ.

The image of a beggar conveys the sense of urgency, dependency, need, attentiveness, vulnerability, trust and hope. Is this how we see our praying?

4 Poverty in prayer

Yesterday, we looked at the act of prayer being likened to a beggar approaching a benefactor. The image conveys a sense of poverty – the person comes to God with nothing – but where does Calvin think that poverty lies? He distinguishes three areas of weakness or poverty. First, external to the believer, are the circumstances in which we find ourselves: 'our present ills', the situations over which we have no control, which bring misery and anxiety. These indicate the fallenness of the world in which we dwell; they impinge upon our well-being and certainly ought to drive us to prayer.

Second, the reformer speaks of our nature – he understands weakness to be inherent in fallen humanity. Throughout his lengthy exposition on prayer, Calvin characteristically accumulates a list of our faults. His too-strong conclusion is that we are 'destitute and devoid of all good things'; but we know our own weaknesses and understand what he means.

Third, he is conscious that we are still sinners – he knows the poverty of our behaviour, depicting us as 'burdened with sins'.

Psalm 130 comes from someone who has reached their limit: 'Out of the depths I cry to you, Lord' (Psalm 130:1); a person who knows their sin: 'If you, Lord, kept a record of sins, Lord, who could stand?' (v. 3; see v. 8). Nevertheless, the psalmist cries to God, waiting attentively for signs of grace in hope of redemption (vv. 1, 5–7). Likewise, the apostle Paul recognises the context of present suffering (Romans 8:18) shared by the whole of creation, the waiting and the hope of salvation (vv. 22–25). And this is the situation in which we pray, where the Holy Spirit graciously enables true prayer to the Father (v. 15).

So we approach God in prayer like beggars, only too aware of our own bankruptcy. But, in warm pastoral application, Calvin urges his readers to be assured that 'prayers poured out by the godly do not depend upon their worthiness'. And Paul similarly speaks of divine enabling, not Christian worthiness: 'the Spirit helps us in our weakness' (v. 26).

What, then, are we to depend on? Divine grace, generosity, faithfulness, Fatherly love, the Spirit's presence and Jesus Christ. That's the basis for authentic prayer.

5 A child asking the Father

Luke 15:11–31

The well-known parable of the lost son, or the expectant father, shows us that when we approach God as Father we do so 'to embrace God's generosity' (in Calvin's words). Recognising his own bankruptcy (vv. 17–19) the miscreant son returns to his father, expecting the minimum, as it were, only to have overwhelmingly generous, undeserved love offered to him on his return (vv. 22–24). Jesus points out that this originates from a deep compassion (v. 20) – perhaps echoing the divine compassion so often underlined in God's relationship with Israel.

The son comes with nothing and the father gives him everything; the son approaches, claiming no status at all, and the father lavishes sonship upon him (v. 22). That is grace demonstrated; grace too big and free to be easily understood (vv. 25–30).

In the context of prayer, Calvin speaks of God the Father and his 'lavish love', even his indulgence. Whatever we, in our poverty, lack is to be found, he says, 'in God, and in our Lord Jesus Christ'. This is a great help in giving us confidence in approaching God: '*We should have no doubt* but that God has a mind to welcome us kindly, is prepared to hear our prayers, and is readily inclined to help us.' The divine riches are abundant and are 'laid up for us with the Heavenly Father'. These are personal ('laid up *for us*'), given to us as adopted children. Calvin is sure that in prayer the Father shows his kindness, grace, mercy and abundant goodness to us; God is promising to help his children, urging them to call on him, anticipating their coming. More than that, though, the Father works in us by the Holy Spirit, stirring us up to pray by attracting us, prompting us, empowering us and even composing prayer for us.

So at the point of recognising his own bankruptcy (vv. 17–19), the son experiences the generosity of his beneficent father (v. 22–24). The father knows all about his son's waywardness but loves him still. He enriches him out of his generosity. Similarly, Calvin sees that this is the pattern of God's love in the context of our praying. We come as children – in the fullness of what that implies; the Father gives and gives again, because of his undeserved grace.

6 All we need is in Jesus Christ

Ephesians 1:3–14

Calvin never tires of emphasising that in Jesus Christ we have everything. This too is the apostle Paul's emphasis as he writes to the Ephesian church. We notice how often he claims Jesus Christ as central to the divine purposes and to their application: we're blessed in Christ, with every spiritual blessing (v. 3); we're chosen in him (vv. 4, 11), predestined in him (v. 5), given grace through him (v. 6); we are redeemed, are included, have hope and are given the Holy Spirit in him (vv. 7, 12–13) – all to the praise of his glory (v. 14).

Christ is central to our experience of God. We cannot approach him without Christ, says Calvin; we are simply not worthy to present ourselves to such a God (see his rules). So the Lord mercifully takes the initiative in the conversation, giving us Jesus Christ, enlivening us by the Holy Spirit, so that all is of grace. Paul speaks of this later in Ephesians: 'For through [Jesus] we... have access to the Father by one Spirit' (2:18). And again: 'In [Jesus] and through faith in him we may approach God with freedom and confidence' (3:12).

The diverse riches that we plead for in prayer and that we experience are to be found only *in* Christ. And, reassuringly, Calvin asserts that the Father *cannot* deny the Son: he is gracious and easily entreated; he is generous to us, even indulgent. We, on our part, should gain confidence, hope and trust from that. As we pray, all we need is in Jesus, God's own Son.

Notice the warmth of the following:

For in Christ [the Lord] offers all happiness in place of our misery, all wealth in place of our neediness; in him he opens to us the heavenly treasures... Whatever we need and whatever we lack is in God, and in our Lord Jesus... It remains for us to seek in him, and in prayers to ask him, what we have learned to be in him.

Pause and ponder the words that indicate our poverty and need, and the image emphasising the Lord's sovereign ability and willingness to help us in our difficulties. Rejoice in Jesus' centrality in all this.

Guidelines

It is John Calvin's understanding that human beings by nature are *dependent beings*. This is so simply because we are created by God; but this fact itself has been underlined by the presence of sin since the fall. Our weakness – fallenness, sins and the circumstances that we cannot manage – is an obstacle to authentic spiritual life, including our prayers. Yet, says Calvin, God has given us all we need in his Son, Jesus Christ. Therefore, we need to *go outside ourselves* – not in any secondary, random direction, for creatures cannot supply our needs, but solely in the direction of the God who *offers* 'all happiness in place of our misery', and *offers* 'all wealth in place of our neediness'. That is, for Calvin, the strength of our weak praying is not so much God strengthening *us*; but the strength we look for is in God himself, or (more exactly) God in Jesus Christ. The reformer does not posit a simple linear model: we are weak; we need God to strengthen *us*. For the reformer, it is somehow more complex than that: it is inherent in a faithful relationship with the Lord that we acknowledge *our* weakness and find *his* strength in Christ.

We do that by acknowledging who God is, and, in so doing, we approach him as a beggar with nothing of our own, and as a child looking for fatherly benevolence. Our prayer starts in the heart – in the place of intimate relationship – but goes outwards from there to seek God in Jesus Christ. It is there that we find abundant grace.

At this point, it might be useful to consider which of Calvin's insights – including his purposes and rules – might help enrich your own experience and practice of prayer. This could be implemented for a month and re-evaluated to see if your spiritual life has been affected.

FURTHER READING

John Calvin, *Institutes of the Christian Religion* (Westminster Press, 1960).

Timothy George, *Theology of the Reformers* (Broadman Press, 1988).

Pamela Moeller, *Calvin's Doxology* (Pickwick, 1997).

Michael Parsons, *Calvin's Preaching on the Prophet Micah* (Edwin Mellen Press, 2006).

Mark 6:30—8

Steve Motyer

Now back to Mark for our third visit of 2018, this time touring the third main division of Mark's story (6:6b—8:30), with a couple of day trips into the next (8:30–38). That tourist metaphor is quite apt, because for these weeks we are on tour with Jesus, following him and his disciples as they move around Galilee from place to place, crossing the lake by boat at least four times (6:32, 45; 8:10, 13), and making excursions outside Israel to Tyre and Sidon on the Mediterranean (7:24, 31) and to Caesarea Philippi (8:27), as well as to the Decapolis (7:31). As we will see, these movements are not incidental to the message of these chapters, but absolutely at its heart.

Jesus is living the lifestyle he commanded for his disciples on mission (6:8–11): travelling around in dependence on God to meet all his needs as he embodies the presence of the kingdom by word and deed – and the disciples are taken along for the ride, seeing and hearing it all. Sometimes food is short (8:16), but Jesus challenges the disciples to learn the lesson of the two feeding miracles that are at the heart of this section of Mark – that of the 5,000 (6:35–44) and the 4,000 (8:1–9). Some scholars, noticing the similarity between these stories, have suggested that they are alternative versions of the same incident. But the repetition is completely germane to Mark's structure and message (here the geography is essential), and so Mark clearly received these stories as distinct, and we will miss his meaning unless we do the same.

The disciples' presence is the key. The section begins and ends with them in private conversation with Jesus (6:30; 8:27), and Mark shows us their *learning process*. Even though they have been out preaching, the disciples still do not 'understand about the loaves, but their hearts were hardened' (6:52). Peter's confession in 8:29 is a great step forward and a climax of the Gospel so far, but he is immediately rebuked for thinking just in a human way (8:33). Mark does not spare the disciples' blushes as they wrestle with their question 'Who then is this?' (4:41). And so he sets up the issues for us, too.

Quotations are from the New Revised Standard Version, although occasionally I have used my own translation.

1 No time to rest

So much is crammed into these five verses! The apostles (the 'sent ones') return from their mission, keen to tell Jesus all about it, and Jesus tries to take them away for a debrief and a rest. This is the counterpart to 2:24, where Jesus gets into trouble for breaking the sabbath rules about work and rest: now we see that he is very keen to balance work and rest, but not according to rule; rather, according to need. Doubtless, like him, the apostles had been preaching and healing on the sabbath while away. Now they need to rest – but clearly not on the sabbath, because otherwise that huge crowd would not have pursued them.

But their rest is sacrificed to the needs of that crowd. As soon as Jesus exits the boat and sees all those people, all thought of time out disappears, swept aside by his compassion for these 'sheep without a shepherd' (v. 34). This is a frequent Old Testament image for people without leadership – either because a leader needs to be appointed (Numbers 27:17), or because the king has died (1 Kings 22:17), or because Israel's so-called leaders are worse than useless (Ezekiel 34:5; Zechariah 10:2–3). With the story of Herod just behind us (6:14–29), and with the emerging picture of the Pharisees showing them as rule-bound and punitive (3:1–6), we can see that Jesus' description of the crowd as 'sheep without a shepherd' fits into the last category here.

Jesus' response to their leaderless state is not to present himself as a 'power-messiah', ready to step into the vacancy. 'He started to teach them a lot' (v. 34), and we know what this means – parable after parable, seeking to grip imagination, heart and mind with the glorious message of the kingdom present among them. This is how God's kingdom comes – not with a ruler of the same type as Herod or the Pharisees, just doing a better job, but with a rule of a new order, one which starts within, in the heart, and works outward to life and society. The disciples are on the journey towards discovering what this means.

It all starts with Jesus' compassion (v. 34). The disciples are learning that the heart of love, which is ready to sacrifice personal comfort and rest for the needs of others, is the keynote of discipleship when Jesus is the master.

2 'You give them something to eat!'

Maybe it would be unfair and cynical to point out – but the disciples know that the place is 'deserted' (v. 35; compare 6:31), so quite where they expect a crowd of 5,000 men (6:44 – plus, presumably, women and children) to find food for sale is puzzling. Are they really trying to rescue a bit of the peace and rest they lost to this crowd – to have some Jesus time for themselves, at last? Pointedly, the same issue is raised by Jesus himself the next time round, but not until *three days* have elapsed (see 8:2). We can surely understand the disciples' frustration; and then certainly empathise with their shock and puzzlement when Jesus tells *them* to solve the problem (v. 37)!

The point is, ministry to others comes first for the disciples of Jesus Christ – a full-orbed ministry both to the mind (the teaching, 6:34) and to the body (the feeding, 6:35–44). The crowd is not sent away to care for their bodies after Jesus has fed their hearts and minds. The kingdom of God is about bodies, too.

First, the disciples must catalogue their resources. This story is not the only miracle in all four Gospels, but Mark alone emphasises the disciples' research: '"How many loaves have you? Go and see." When they had found out…' (v. 38). Interestingly, five loaves and two fish are not sufficient for the disciples, let alone the whole crowd. But – like the mustard seed which can become a tree sheltering flocks of birds (4:30–32) – the kingdom of God can transform the resources Jesus' disciples bring, provided they are willing (a) to bring them, and (b) to act in crazy obedience when Jesus starts telling them what to do with them.

The disciples' response to Jesus' initial crazy suggestion is quite sharply worded (v. 37) – disrespectful, even: 'Are you telling us to go and spend thousands of pounds buying food, and simply give it to them?' ('Two hundred denarii' is about eight months' wages for an ordinary working man.) Paradoxically, in view of the miracle to follow, Jesus' reply points them away from the impossible, to focus instead on the *possible*: how much do you have already? Take stock, and start with that…

The kingdom principle is that we always have enough to do God's will, right now: and sometimes he calls us to crazy acts of faith that defy common sense.

3 Food in the desert

This story, so simply told, is full of overtones that hum suggestively. For instance, Mark's first readers would surely have heard tones of the Eucharist murmuring in verse 41: Jesus breaks bread, gives thanks and feeds his people. And that tune connects with others that form a delicate counterpoint weaving in the background here.

The Eucharist was instituted at Jesus' last Passover, at which he gave a new focus to that memorial meal; and the 'green grass' on the hillside here (v. 39) suggests that this feeding happens at Passover time – a connection that John makes explicit (John 6:4). Passover was the annual memorial of the exodus, when God's people were delivered from slavery in Egypt and a new covenant was made, sealed by a meal at which the elders of Israel 'beheld God, and ate and drank' (Exodus 24:11). And the Passover also recalled the desert wanderings, when Israel was miraculously fed by God, sustained by the manna for 40 years (Exodus 16:35). So here again is a great crowd of Israelites, in a 'deserted place' (6:31, 35), being miraculously fed, at Passover time, in an act which points ahead to that later feeding at which Jesus will declare the inauguration of 'the new covenant in my blood' (Luke 22:20).

Israel's Lord is present again, to feed and satisfy his people! Even the twelve baskets of leftovers suggest that this is a meal for more than those present – for all twelve tribes, in fact. Some Jewish traditions taught that, when the Messiah came, he would again feed Israel as Moses did in the wilderness, and that this miracle would be the sign of his arrival. Did anyone think of that, as they sat in groups of 50 or 100 on that grassy slope? The extraordinary thing is that the story is told in such a low-key way that it is unclear whether any of the crowd realised that the feast had started with five loaves and two fish. There are no statements of amazement after this miracle, unlike with others (e.g. 2:12). We see the whole action from the disciples' perspective, and are left at the end to wonder what they make of it. Do they hear these echoes of the exodus, the covenant, the manna? It must have been an amazing experience, to share the food round that huge crowd, knowing how it started. Where does it leave them?

4 Leading his people through

Mark 6:45–52

This is a strange story. It starts oddly with Jesus compelling his disciples into the boat (v. 45 – Mark uses a strong Greek word). It feels as though something must be enacted – and indeed this story of Jesus walking on the water stands out among his miracles because it doesn't have an obvious quality of rescue from some human need. The disciples were 'straining at the oars' but not about to sink in a storm (v. 48). And, rather than heading straight for the boat, Jesus 'intended to pass them by', until his very presence created the need for rescue, when they spotted this ghostly figure drifting past and became terrified (vv. 49–50).

What's going on? Again, the Old Testament comes to our aid. Mark drops a hint in verse 51 by telling us that the disciples were 'utterly astounded' by what happened (the Greek is very strong – 'absolutely gobsmacked' would do better) because 'they had not understood about the loaves'. In other words, Mark suggests a hidden connection between this water-walking miracle and the feeding of the 5,000: understand one, and you won't be surprised by the other. What's the link? It emerges when we reflect that the exodus was marked not only by the Passover and food in the desert, but also by the crossing of the Red Sea, when God led his people through the waters. Looking back on this people-forming event, the psalmist sings, 'Your way was through the sea, your path through the mighty waters; yet your footprints were unseen. You led your people like a flock…' (Psalm 77:19–20).

It's all happening again! Jesus forges a pathway through the sea, like Israel's God of old, moving faster through the wind and waves than the disciples can row. They are terrified to witness this re-enactment, because they do not spot its significance – but by receiving Jesus into the boat they do at least signal their willingness to get on board with this recreation of God's people, this symbolic remaking of Israel through another exodus sea-taming. 'I am' in verse 50 (literal translation of 'It is I') might even echo the divine name 'I am who I am' which stands over the whole exodus event (Exodus 3:14).

The last note is sobering – 'but their hearts were hardened' (v. 52). The insiders are like those outside (see 4:12). Can hard hearts be softened? How?

5 Off course or on track?

They set off to cross to Bethsaida (6:45) – the north-east shore of Galilee – but land at Gennesaret (v. 53: the western shore, south of Capernaum). What's this about? Scholars suggest either that Mark doesn't know the local geography or that he has inexpertly edited disparate stories together. But if we simply allow his narrative to flow, the boat ends up at an unintended destination (perhaps because of those annoying headwinds in 6:48). Why would Mark subtly indicate this? We could read it symbolically, because at the moment the disciples are missing their goal in a bigger sense, also. They are supposed to be grasping 'the mystery of God's kingdom' (4:11), but are just not getting it – and with that extraordinary diagnosis of 'hardened hearts' (v. 52), what hope is there? Can they ever arrive at this bigger Bethsaida?

The disciples are now witnesses to one of those dramas so typical of Jesus' ministry. What do they make of it? Crowds of people bring their sick, trying to anticipate where they will find Jesus so that the sick (or their friends and relatives – Mark is ambiguous) might simply touch the hem of his cloak: 'And all who touched him were healed' (v. 56).

Where have we met that before? Of course, back in 5:27–28, where the woman with 'the issue of blood' did the same – and the vital thing was the *faith* with which she touched Jesus' cloak. 'Your faith has healed you,' he said. 'Go in peace!' (5:34). Here we see the same on a bigger scale – and through Mark's few words we can feel the tremulous anguish and hope with which those crowds of people also trusted that Jesus could heal their loved ones.

Can hard hearts be mended like broken bodies? This is the question lurking underneath the narrative here, through the unmentioned presence of the disciples. There is something wonderfully true, psychologically, in Mark's acknowledgement that puzzlement and faith can exist together: the disciples are following Jesus, even acting as his ambassadors (6:7), though they don't yet understand him. They *believe*, even alongside the brutal diagnosis of 'hardened hearts', which puts them in a bracket with Pharaoh (Exodus 7:13) and the Pharisees (Mark 3:5) – and also with Israel experiencing exodus but being tempted to worship a golden calf (Deuteronomy 9:13; 10:16). So once again we end with this question: can hard hearts be healed? How?

6 Human tradition – and God's word

Mark 7:1–8

At first sight, it looks like a complete change of direction in the story at this point. Centre-stage now are the Pharisees, and a debate about purity – with a long explanation (probably especially for Gentile readers) of how issues of purity impacted daily life for the Pharisees and all Jews influenced by their teaching (vv. 3–4). This purity was not about hygiene; this was about bringing all of life into conformity with God's word (for instance Leviticus 14—5 and Numbers 19), requiring elaborate ritual washings which would ensure that the purity required for the temple was maintained in every home.

But Jesus says that this is all just 'human tradition', uncommanded by God (v. 8). And that takes us under the surface to the underlying question: who has the right to interpret and apply scripture authoritatively? Jesus speaks 'with authority, not like the scribes' (1:22), and we have just seen him deliberately re-enacting the great exodus events, especially the feeding in the desert and the crossing of the Red Sea. The next thing in the exodus story was arrival at Sinai and the giving of the law (Exodus 19—23). Jesus now claims the right to explain 'the commandment of God' (v. 8) and to apply it – and this is the agenda for the whole of chapter 7, as we will see.

What is going on when people use God's commands as a basis for merely human ideas and prescriptions? This takes us into another underlying issue, signalled by the quotation of Isaiah 29:13 in verses 6–7: the *heart* as the place of true, or false, worship. This gives us another connection with chapter 6, especially the dramatic 6:52. Worship can look great on the outside, fulfilling all the 'rules', but the heart can be miles away. This is not about minds wandering during services, but about motivations which are human-centred rather than God-centred, so that worship is devoted to human goals rather than to God himself. There is huge opportunity for self-deception here, because human motivations can so easily dress up in religious garb and come strongly reinforced by 'normal' expected social practices, as here.

The disciples are clearly happy to dispense with the full rigour of the Pharisaic washings (v. 2) – but how are *their* hearts at the moment? Still hard? What kind of worship can they offer? First, they need to learn about 'the word of God', as we will see next week.

Guidelines

Reflection on this week's readings raises a challenging question about the quality of our worship. Could Jesus quote Isaiah 29:13 over us, also: 'This people honours me with their lips, but their hearts are far from me'? What constitutes a heart close to God?

This week's segment of Mark gives us two answers to this question, both of them negative. First, the heart close to God will not be 'utterly astounded' (6:51) by the power of Jesus to multiply loaves and walk on water. Turning this into a positive, the heart close to God will be ready to recognise the power of God at work in Jesus, and to trust him to provide for his people and to bring them safely home, whatever storms may threaten us. (This is how the story in 6:48–52 was read in the early church – as an allegory of the church of Christ safe in the storms, which Jesus treads beneath his feet.)

Second, the heart close to God will not be ensnared by human traditions masquerading as the commandment of God – or, to put it positively, the heart close to God will be ready to question all religious traditions, however well established, in the light of a fresh reading of scripture and a new appreciation of God's word. We will see more of what this means next week, as Mark develops this theme further.

So the heart close to God may need to be ready to choose uncertainty and change over religious certainty and stable tradition, deliberately stepping *into* the storm as the Saviour forges a path through the waves – not a comfortable choice, but the only option for true disciples compelled to get into the boat (6:45)! The Pharisees and Jesus represent alternative visions of the people of God, one resting in the security of known tradition and established ways, the other emphasising the need for faith to embrace new ways and unknown paths. True worship is marked by the latter!

1 Plastic religion

Mark 7:9–13

Jesus is scathing about the capacity of these legal experts to turn scripture on its head while still apparently being faithful and devout. Their whole life is in theory dedicated to bringing each detail of behaviour into conformity with God's word. But Jesus looks at the heart motivating their intellectual debates. He chooses one particular issue and discerns the avarice he later lists as one of the 'impurities from within' (7:22).

The debate concerned whether oaths should take precedence over duty to parents. The law says that 'when a man makes a vow to the Lord, or swears an oath to bind himself by a pledge, he shall not break his word; he shall do according to all that proceeds out of his mouth' (Numbers 30:2; see also Deuteronomy 23:21–23). So if a man vows to give to the temple the money or goods with which he might otherwise have supported his elderly parents, the scribal view was that the vow must be inviolable – even though people could make such vows to take effect on their death, and thus retain use of the money and goods while they still lived and avoid losing them to fulfil their duty to their parents.

The human tradition in this case is the legal judgement that, in obedience to Numbers 30:2, vows must always trump other duties, whatever they are. Jesus is horrified: this amounts to nullifying God's word, because the duty to care for parents is so important, expressed in the ten commandments themselves and in the holiness code that follows in Exodus (v. 10; Exodus 20:12; 21:17).

Jesus is clear that human tradition deeply affects the way we read and interpret the Bible. And he is also clear that, for good or ill, our *hearts* – our vital centre of emotion, desire, reason and will – are the key factor in shaping our judgement about what scripture teaches and how we should obey it. Interestingly, these two factors – the role of tradition and of personal stance – have become key centres in modern debates in hermeneutics about the process of interpretation. Unlike the emphasis in contemporary hermeneutics, however, Jesus asks us to be deeply self-critical about our personal stance. Are our hearts hard, too? Are we motivated by any of those impurities in 7:21–22? How do these affect our hearing of God's word?

2 Real impurity

Jesus now addresses the issue of purity raised in 7:1–5. Actually, 7:6–13 has addressed the first half of the Pharisees' question in 7:5 (the issue of 'the tradition of the elders'), and now Jesus turns to the second part of their question, to do with eating with 'defiled hands'. He addresses the wider crowd with a strange statement which Mark calls a 'parable' in verse 17: we are defiled, he says, not by what goes into us, but by what comes out.

What does this mean, and how does it address the issue of ritual hand-washing? No wonder the disciples ask Jesus about it, when once again the indoor seminar convenes. Jesus' initial response is very revealing: 'So – are you too without understanding?' (v. 18). They are *supposed* to understand the parables, which contain 'the mystery of the kingdom' (4:11). These are the underlying issues throughout this section: whether the disciples are getting it (or whether their hearts are still hardened like those of the Pharisees – remember 6:52), and what's involved in softening hard hearts and giving real understanding of Jesus.

So the heart is the key theme here. *Hearts* are the source of impurity, says Jesus, not grubby hands or the wrong sort of food. Ritual purity comes as a package, with all its elements connected by the belief that people become defiled before God by a range of wrong actions or inactions – e.g. touching a corpse, failing to wash correctly or eating foods forbidden by the law. Jesus cuts beneath all this to the state of the heart, which is untouched by the foods we eat (v. 19).

There is plenty of room for debate about the interpretation of scripture, as we saw yesterday. But here's the rub: there is no doubt at all that scripture forbids the consumption of certain foods (e.g. Deuteronomy 14:3–21). *So, having criticised the Pharisees for exalting their traditions over obeying God's commands, Jesus now overthrows one of God's explicit commandments by 'declaring all foods clean' (v. 19b).*

Well, that is Mark's interpretation of Jesus' teaching! The bracketed comment in verse 19 is his aside, popped in for the sake of his immediate readers. This may not have been obvious to the disciples and those who heard the 'parable' that day. But Mark wants us to be in no doubt. This, he says, is what Jesus' teaching means. What? How can this be? Come back tomorrow!

3 Something is rotten in the heart...

Mark 7:20–23

We need to bear in mind yesterday's shocker – Mark's aside about Jesus 'declaring all foods clean' (v. 19b). Why does Mark see something so radical in Jesus' teaching about the evil capacity of the human heart? A string of Jewish heroes had faced martyrdom rather than being forced to eat pork. To eat pork would have been to deny their whole identity as Jews. Yes, that is indeed the point: tomorrow we will see the full implications of this, as Jesus extends the blessings of the kingdom of God to a Gentile. The food laws were one of the vital symbols of Israel's uniqueness as God's people, separating them from the rotten, defiled Gentile world. With the arrival of the kingdom, Mark is saying, these barriers are coming down, and 'impure' Gentiles are being welcomed just on the basis of their faith in Jesus. Jewish identity is changing.

To prepare the way for that radical move, Jesus first shifts the focus of our need, as human beings. We need to be saved, not from ritual impurity contracted by eating the wrong foods or not washing hands and pots, but from the impurity of our own hearts. The right foods just don't cut it. 'Evil intentions' come from within (v. 21) – the word translated 'intentions' covers also the reasoning and decision-making process that underlie the intentions we develop.

To press the point home, Jesus then gives a depressing list of twelve examples of inner impurity: the first six are in the plural, which gives the flavour 'acts of...', and then the final six are in the singular (beginning with 'deceit'), pointing to the impure qualities that underlie the actions covered by the first six.

What a sad list! Twelve, of course, is the number of Israel, and might point in that direction, like the twelve baskets in 6:43. But we cannot point the finger at the same time! This is *universal* human neediness, a catalogue of vices and failings which cause conflict, agony and loss the world over. The last in the list – folly – seems to underlie all the others (the terrible counterpart of 'wisdom' in Proverbs), and to point to the present state of the disciples, who just can't see the obvious about Jesus.

Can we be saved from this inner rottenness? If these twelve impurities match those twelve baskets of life-giving bread, there could be hope. God's kingdom is present in Jesus, with new life-giving power.

4 A heart of love and faith

Mark 7:24–30

What a fascinating story. The basic point is clear – Jesus is breaking down the barrier between Jews and Gentiles (the ultimate division made by the covenant with Israel, and symbolised by distinctive things like the food laws), so that Gentiles too, despite their 'uncleanness', may receive the blessings of Israel's Messiah. The 'unclean spirit' possessed by the little girl (v. 25) underlines this point vividly – Gentile 'uncleanness' is being swept away.

This breaking down of the division between Jews and Gentiles will become the glorious heart of Paul's gospel and ministry. So why the reluctance here? Why does Jesus give the distraught mother such a rude brush-off (v. 27), even referring to her obliquely as a 'dog' – a regular insulting Jewish description of Gentiles?

Paul also believed that the gospel was 'for the Jew *first*' (Romans 1:16, my italics), and that is clearly an emphasis here, too, underlined particularly in Matthew's version of this story where Jesus explains his dismissive attitude by saying, 'I was sent only to the lost sheep of the house of Israel' (Matthew 15:24). But that can't be the whole story, for Jesus changes his mind and helps the woman – and indeed Mark clearly thinks that this move into the Gentile world is central to the work of the kingdom. So why does Jesus speak so sharply?

I find it helpful to look at the story from a psychotherapy angle. Jesus clearly had empathy by the bucketful – that is, the capacity instinctively to know what was being felt and thought by those he met. Jesus' words in verse 27, I believe, mirror back to the woman what she feels about herself as she approaches him. (Such empathic mirroring is a key psychotherapy technique.) She has internalised that description of herself as a 'dog'. Jesus probes her heart, exposing this degraded sense of herself, and allowing her to express her feisty determination not to let that low judgement stop her from appealing to Jesus for her daughter. She too accepts that Jesus came for the Jew first, but she also believes that the Gentiles may come to Jesus too! With his one razor-sharp comment, Jesus elicits her whole heart, particularly her faith towards him, as well as her love for her daughter. And she illustrates also the truth of Jesus' words in Luke 10:13!

What's coming out of *her* heart? This 'impure' Gentile reveals faith and love way beyond that of the disciples themselves.

5 Deafness dismissed

Mark 7:31–37

Jesus' miracles, as we have seen, can capture and express truths about the kingdom, just like his parables. This one is no exception. This deaf man has his hearing restored just a couple of paragraphs after Jesus' appeal to the crowd, 'Hear me, all of you…!' (7:14). And we remember the vital 'Let anyone with ears to hear listen!' (4:9, 23), which in some early manuscripts is repeated in this chapter (7:16). Hearing means much more than the capacity to register sound. True hearing means understanding. Without understanding, we might as well be deaf. Deaf ears go with dull minds, according to Isaiah 6:9–10, quoted in Mark 4:12.

So this story signifies a lot, when the deaf man has his hearing restored – and with it his speech. Jesus can give hearing in every sense, we gather. He can enable his hard-hearted disciples (indeed, anyone) to 'hear' him truly, to understand his parables and thus *speak* with authority about him.

It is surely significant, also, that this healing takes place in a Gentile area. From Tyre on the Mediterranean coast Jesus heads north to Sidon, and then heads back inland to the Decapolis (v. 31), a large Greek-speaking area west, north-west and south-west of Galilee. It was so called after the ten Greek cities which were the focal points for this area, which stretched as far as Damascus, according to the Roman historian Pliny. Many Jews lived here, but only a section of north Decapolis fell within the tetrarchy of Herod Philip, and many Gentiles also lived in this very mixed area. Mark leaves it open whether this deaf and dumb man is a Gentile or not – clearly it doesn't matter to him. He records Jesus' Aramaic word of healing, but immediately translates it (v. 34). Nor does it matter whether the watching crowd are Jewish or Gentile or both. Whichever, they disobey Jesus' instructions and 'zealously proclaim' the healing, 'astounded beyond measure' by what he has done (vv. 36–37).

In their final verdict, 'He has done everything well; he makes even the deaf to hear and the mute to speak' (v. 37). The vital words 'deaf' and 'mute' are in the plural. This healing is not a one-off, they are saying; there is hope now for all the 'deaf', whether Jews or Gentiles, because a new power is in the world: the power of God's kingdom in Christ.

6 Loaves and Fish 2

Mark 8:1–10

Sequels usually have the same cast but a different storyline. But this sequel is simply an action rerun of Loaves and Fish 1 in 6:35–44. What's the point? Some scholars fasten on to the small differences between the stories, looking for some significance – 4,000 rather than 5,000 people; seven loaves rather than five; seven baskets of leftovers rather than twelve. But these details simply seem to underline that this really is a rerun of the same miracle, at a different time and place.

Perhaps that's part of the point – the *place*. Jesus is still in the Decapolis. He crosses to the western (more Jewish) shore of Galilee after this feeding of the crowd (v. 10). Loaves and Fish 1 – followed by Jesus walking on the lake – drew on strong Old Testament symbolism rooted in the covenant with Israel, and seemed to suggest a glorious new covenant in the offing. So when Loaves and Fish 2 runs the same symbolism for a mixed crowd of Jews and Gentiles, what is the message? As for the Syrophoenician woman in 7:24–30, the covenant is being opened up to Gentiles, and Israel's food is available for all.

Once again, of course, the symbolism of the Eucharist would have been strongly evoked for Mark's first readers, who were probably members of mixed Jewish-Gentile congregations. And the repetition of 'were filled' (v. 8; 6:42; also 7:27, 'let the children *be filled* first') points to lavish supply, in a hand-to-mouth society where people rarely ate until they could eat no more. God in Christ is not about just helping us get by. There is more than enough to sustain us, even if we have to starve for three days first (v. 2)! This crowd well illustrates the truth of Matthew 6:33: 'Strive first for the kingdom of God and his righteousness, and all these things will be given to you as well.'

Where are the disciples in this? Once again, the story is told from their point of view, but we hear nothing from them after their sceptical question in verse 4. What do they think? Professor Morna Hooker points out that their question is exactly what sceptical Israel might have said to Moses, faced with starving in the wilderness (Exodus 16:2). Are the disciples still in the same puzzled, unsure place as in 6:37, 52? We are about to find out.

Guidelines

Looking back over this week's readings, we have met several themes. We've seen the way in which religion can be taken hostage to human agendas and desires, and the way religion can be used to cover over some very dark stuff in the depths of human motivation; positively, we've seen the need to expose all that inner impurity, to let the light of Christ shine on it – and perhaps especially to let Jesus expose our tribal instincts, to help us to cross boundaries and reach out to the unacceptable 'other', whoever that might be. (Matthew's version of the story about the Syrophoenician woman shows *the disciples* being very scornful and rejecting of her – Matthew 15:21–28.) And we've touched again on the need to let God do the completely unexpected and impossible – and the way in which 'can't' simply isn't a word in the divine vocabulary. If a massive crowd needs feeding and he wants to do it, then even our tiny resources will be sufficient, provided we are ready to launch out in obedience.

Behind it all runs the theme of Jesus' patient tutelage of his strangely uncomprehending disciples. They are silent through this section, except for their questions in 7:17 and 8:4. How patient Jesus is with them! (We will see much more of this next week.) I am deeply struck by his readiness to let them be hard of heart, and to move at their own speed towards understanding and real faith, even though at the same time he is pictured as one able to restore hearing and speech with a simple touch and word of command. How does this speak to our relationship with those still on the way to believing? How should we be with them?

As you look back over these varied themes, let one of them stand out for you and prompt your reflection and prayer to round off your experience of Mark this week.

1 Proof?

Mark 8:11–13

It's fair enough to ask for proof of his claims, isn't it? Why then does Jesus refuse to give the Pharisees the 'sign' they ask for? In the eyes of many, we can imagine, this refusal would be tantamount to disproof. Clearly, they would conclude, he cannot provide the proof needed, and therefore refuses. Similarly, in our day, many have embraced atheism because there seems to be no proof of the claims made about Jesus, or any of the other theistic religions. And many who follow Jesus can still harbour doubts for the same reason. Why doesn't God give a clear sign of his existence?

Jesus gives a deep sigh and asks, 'Why does this generation seek a sign?' It might be reasonable to ask for proof, but there is huge irony in this question – because there have already been signs aplenty, not least the amazing feeding that just took place on the other side of the lake. The Pharisees just haven't *seen* them. If told rumours about the feeding, they might reply, 'But we weren't there!' – to which the response is 'No, you weren't, were you…'

The point is: to those who opt in and commit themselves to follow, the signs become gradually clearer (though we are still not quite sure where the disciples themselves are on this scale). But if you sit outside and ask for proof, it cannot be given. 'No sign will be given to this generation,' says Jesus, not because he is reluctant to provide one, but because 'this generation' cannot *receive* signs given to them. A 'generation' is a culture with fixed ways of discernment that filter out non-standard evidence, especially ways of receiving God and spiritual perspectives (see Deuteronomy 32:5; Psalm 95:10; Hebrews 4:2). The evidence, although demanded, is filtered out of perception and therefore denied.

All Jesus can do is sadly re-embark and depart (v. 13). Ironically, his departure is itself a 'sign' to them. If they came with him – then the story might be different. But we must not only point the finger at this 'generation' of Pharisees. In what ways might we be filtering out the reality of God from our perception, not allowing ourselves truly to see the 'signs' of his kingdom and presence? In what ways are the disciples still doing this, in Mark's narrative? The next paragraph puts them, and us, on the spot.

2 What makes your dough rise?

Mark 8:14–21

The first feeding miracle was followed by a lake crossing which ended with Mark's horrifying comment about the disciples' hardness of heart (6:52). Now, after the second feeding miracle, the disciples are back in the boat, and once again the focus is the hardness of their hearts – but now in the form of a question: 'Do you still not perceive or understand? Are your hearts hardened?' (v. 17). Then Jesus quotes some words from Jeremiah, from the bad old days when Israel was accused of abandoning her God in favour of other gods: 'Having eyes do you not see, and having ears do you not hear?' (v. 18; Jeremiah 5:21; see also Ezekiel 12:2). The disciples could be like faithless, rebellious Israel – no better, in fact, than the Pharisees and Herod.

The 'yeast' of the Pharisees – what floats their boat, to change the metaphor – is an unyielding faithfulness to their tradition, which makes them (and us) reject anything new. The yeast of Herod (see 6:17–29) is devotion to worldly power and self-sufficiency, which makes him (and us) reject a word of God that tells us we are weak and dependent. Prompted by their lack of food in the boat – a problem for which neither religious tradition nor self-sufficiency has a solution – the disciples face this question: what kind of yeast will make their dough rise, metaphorically? Are they ready for a new life of dependence and faith in Jesus the Messiah?

The Pharisees and Herod would simply fire accusation and scorn at the disciples for their forgetfulness. But Jesus gently reminds them of the two feeding miracles (vv. 19–20). He will not ram faith down their throats. It cannot be forced in from outside – it must be born within, in a softening of hard hearts (the positive counterpart to what Jesus said about impurity in 7:15). His questions probe, and tease, and cajole, with love.

'Do you not yet understand?' (v. 21). What precisely should they be understanding now? It's more than just becoming intellectually convinced that Jesus is the Messiah; it's also developing the kind of faith in him which would impact their approach to this practical problem: no bread in the boat, and a whole day at sea. Faith always shows itself in relation to life's surprises, dilemmas, fears, pains and disasters: that's when it really becomes clear what makes our dough rise.

3 The blind see! (1)

This is another of those lovely symbolic miracles. Jesus' two acute questions in 8:18 look in opposite directions – the second back to the healing in 7:32–37, and the first forward to this story. Once again people bring a disabled man to Jesus with a request for healing (v. 22; 7:32), and Jesus takes him away from the public space (v. 23a; 7:33a), so that the encounter is without distraction, and also (perhaps especially) so that it is not a quasi-magic performance. In both cases, the healing is then described in vivid physical terms – hands, fingers, touching, spittle, ears, tongues and eyes. But a difference emerges after the healing actions: in the case of the blind man, Jesus echoes his question in verse 18 to the disciples as he asks, 'Can you see anything?' (v. 23b).

This is the only healing miracle which occurs exclusively in Mark, and is not taken up by any other Gospel. Perhaps this is because of the oddness of what happens next – maybe particularly because of the implication that Jesus didn't get the healing right at first and needed to have another go. 'I see people, but I see them as trees, walking,' replies the man (v. 24). Jesus then repeats the healing action and, Mark says, the man then 'looked closely, and was restored and saw everything clearly' (v. 25).

A two-stage healing! First the man's sight is repaired, *and then as a separate action his perception is healed* – and it is this second stage which constitutes the real restoration. He learns not just to see, but also rightly to *interpret* what he sees. He can now tell the difference between people and trees! This maps straight on to the experience of the disciples: they have seen what Jesus has been doing – but have they really *seen*? Has sight been accompanied by true perception? Or are they effectively still blind, like the Pharisees to whom no sign can be given (8:12)?

This story portrays Jesus as the source of healing in the fullest sense – he can restore the power to discern, as well as the power to see. But how does he give true understanding? He looks a little powerless as he pleads with his disciples in 8:17–21, even though we don't hear an answer from the disciples at that point. What will make the difference for them – and, indeed, for us? How is faith born?

4 The blind see! (2)

Mark 8:27–30

Peter's famous confession at Caesarea Philippi brings this section of Mark's Gospel to a rousing conclusion. It is a remarkable shift!

Once again, Jesus and his disciples are on the road, travelling north from the Jewish heartlands to their fringes around Caesarea Philippi, which lay about 40 miles north of Capernaum, just below Mount Hermon. 'On the road,' says Mark (v. 27), Jesus broaches the subject of his own identity, and hears from the disciples all the options which were being canvassed right back at the start of this section – see 6:14–16. Has nothing changed? Then Jesus asks the million-dollar question: 'But you – who do you say that I am?' He hears Peter's response, given on behalf of them all: 'You are the Christ!' In Matthew, Peter's response is fuller – 'You are the Christ, the Son of the living God!' (Matthew 16:16) – and some early manuscripts of Mark give this fuller version also.

This is a clear answer, at last, to the disciples' question in 4:41 – 'Who then is this?' – though they have much yet to learn about what it means for Jesus to be 'the Christ'. But most fascinating is Mark's presentation of the process whereby the disciples have come to this conviction. Over these chapters, their faith has stumbled and stuttered, but now it grandly emerges. What made the difference, at this moment on the road north? Faith grows within, and at some point – which could seem quite random – it bursts into conscious awareness. For one of the UK's most prominent 20th-century converts, this moment occurred 'one sunny morning' during a drive to Whipsnade Zoo. 'When we set out,' wrote C.S. Lewis in *Surprised by Joy*, 'I did not believe that Jesus Christ is the Son of God, and when we reached the zoo I did. Yet I had not exactly spent the journey in thought' – though he had for some time been wrestling with issues of faith and unbelief. As a result, 'Wallaby Wood, with the birds singing overhead and the bluebells underfoot and the wallabies hopping all round one, was almost Eden come again.' I wonder whether the disciples felt like that, when they finally confessed Jesus as the Christ to him and to each other.

Typically Jesus silences them (v. 30) – but now we understand that the kingdom of God will prove its presence gradually and quietly, and not by forceful trumpeting!

5 'Then he began...'

The second half of Mark's Gospel begins at this point, signalled by this opening phrase, 'Then he began...' Something new starts at this moment – the announcement of Jesus' coming rejection, torture and death at the hands of the authorities, and the story of the fulfilment of this prediction. Jesus repeats it in 9:12, in 9:31, in 10:33–34 and in 10:45; and then, with his arrival in Jerusalem in chapter 11, it starts to be fulfilled.

This is exactly *not* what Peter thought should happen to 'Jesus the Christ'! In making that confession of who Jesus is, he and the other disciples had a pretty clear idea of what it meant: the Messiah will cleanse God's people by bringing God's justice to Israel, delivering her from her enemies (the Romans) and establishing Israel in security around her temple and holy city, Jerusalem. In all likelihood, this will begin – as with other messianic claimants in the first century – by raising an army and marching on Jerusalem.

So this talk of the Messiah being killed cannot be! Again, Peter acts as spokesman for all the disciples as he takes Jesus aside and begins to rebuke him, just as Jesus rebuked the demon in 1:25 and the sea in 4:39. But in turn, Jesus rebukes Peter in front of the whole group of disciples (v. 33), amazingly calling him 'Satan' for voicing a purely human idea of the Messiah, and not *God's* idea. It is not going to be easy for Peter to understand and accept that the Messiah must die.

It is still deeply counterintuitive. Governments the world over are animated by what Professor Walter Wink has called 'the myth of redemptive violence' – that is, the view that violent force is the essential engine of justice, backed up by armies and criminal justice systems enforced by state power. Of course, freedom movements like Peter's first-century Jewish messianism take the same view. Wink calls it a 'myth' because it is a story we constantly tell ourselves about the world, reinforced through countless Hollywood blockbusters (and cartoons) which graphically celebrate 'redemptive violence' in action. The goodies zap the baddies; they don't die for them.

Jesus' teaching that it is necessary (v. 31, 'must') points to God's very different plan. There must be 'great suffering' and death, but not that of the baddies who deserve it; rather, 'the Son of Man' must suffer and die. What does this mean? Why?

6 Carrying the cross

Jesus doesn't just teach the unpalatable truth of a suffering and dying Messiah – he then makes it the core theme in his view of discipleship: '"If any of you want to come the way I'm going," he said, "you must say 'no' to your own selves, pick up your cross, and follow me"' (v. 34, Tom Wright's translation). This is an incredibly moving and powerful image: everyone in that listening crowd had seen squads of Roman soldiers leading a procession of condemned men carrying their own crosses to the place of execution. (The Romans used crucifixion, and the vivid threat of it, as a terrible way of enforcing their power.) 'Carrying your own cross' is a most powerful picture of a life finished – all ambition, desire and will obliterated by the authority of another who compels this last act of carrying one's own cross before execution.

Jesus asks his disciples *voluntarily* to take up this position of 'losing their lives' to follow him (v. 35), because we will lose our lives anyway if we seek to preserve them by our own effort and for our own ends. This amounts to a promise that those who give up their lives to follow him will be saved *from death*. The little parable in verse 36 is illustrated by the longer one in Luke 12:13–21, which underlines the uselessness of vast wealth and holds out the prospect instead of being 'rich towards God' (Luke 12:21) if we guard against greed and follow the Lord.

This paragraph begins and ends with Jesus referring to himself as 'the Son of Man' – first concerning his sufferings (v. 31), then concerning his coming in glory (v. 38). He has used this name only twice thus far in the Gospel (2:10, 28), but now it will be his favourite self-designation, used twelve times in the second half of Mark, and always with reference either to suffering or to glory (suffering: 10:33, 45; 14:41; glory: 13:26, 14:62). For these are the two sides of one coin in Mark's theology. Like Jesus the Christ, we suffer in order to enter glory, and our glory is to bear suffering in his name. It would have been easy for the disciples to reject such a shame-filled life, following a crucified Messiah – but Jesus reminds them that much more is at stake than their reputation here and now (v. 38).

Guidelines

The surprise involved in Jesus' presentation of a *suffering* Messiah is enormous, particularly because he then turns the suffering Messiah into the pattern of discipleship. The Messiah doesn't suffer so that others might be spared it. Rather, he calls us to embrace a life in which our desire for ease and freedom from pain is banished in favour of following him through suffering and loss, if he leads us that way. It would be appropriate to reflect on what this might mean for you, at this point in your life.

The American missionary Jim Elliot, who with four others was martyred in Ecuador in 1956 by the Huaorani people he was seeking to reach, famously wrote in his journal, 'He is no fool who gives what he cannot keep to gain that which he cannot lose.' This pinpoints a feature of Christian life and theology quite unique among world religions – the view that, in God's economy, the weak are more powerful than the strong, loss is the way to gain, 'the poor in spirit' (Matthew 5:3) are blessed rather than the mighty, and suffering and death are the place of victory. The 19th-century philosopher Nietzsche has been followed by many in despising this exaltation of weakness – and it does indeed run counter to a culture which sees power as our primary defence against injustice and the malice of others.

How do you think that this key Christian focus on the cross as the place of redemption should affect our view of the world today – both in terms of the big political picture, and in relation to the challenge of embodying a Christian witness with integrity in each locality? There are no easy answers here, but Mark would surely assume that, in one way or another – like Jesus – Christians will stand alongside the poor and the low in the name of God's kingdom.

FURTHER READING

Conrad Gempf, *Jesus Asked. What he wanted to know* (Zondervan, 2003).

Conrad Gempf, *Mealtime Habits of the Messiah: 40 encounters with Jesus* (Zondervan, 2005).

Morna Hooker, *The Gospel According to St Mark* (A & C Black, 1981).

C.S. Lewis, *Surprised by Joy* (Collins, 2012; first published 1955).

Tom Wright, *Mark for Everyone* (SPCK, 2001).

Sharing possessions in the New Testament and today

Fiona Gregson

Over the last 20 centuries, Christians have shared with one another and others in a variety of ways – whether through monastic communities, church mutual care funds, shared households, or provision of healthcare and relief in hardship. This sharing has been about building communities of fellowship and love as well as providing for needs. We are daily faced with all kinds of needs – our own and other people's: how do we respond to the person begging on the street, to the friend who we know is in need, to those who are experiencing hardship further afield?

The New Testament includes a number of examples of sharing, from sharing between small groups of people in one location to providing for those affected by famine and persecution in a different location. These examples show a pattern of distinctively Christian ways of sharing when compared with how other groups in the first century shared with one another. Over the next two weeks, we will look at some of the New Testament examples, and at how we might learn from them about sharing with one another.

Quotations are from the New International Version (Anglicised).

5–11 November

1 The first disciples

Luke 5:1–11, 27–32; John 4:1–8

Right at the beginning of his ministry, we see Jesus calling people into community and relationship – to follow him as his disciples. Discipleship was not unusual in first-century Palestine. Rabbis would have disciples, although most of the evidence is of disciples choosing their rabbis, and, while there is evidence of rabbis in the desert, there is little evidence of rabbis and disciples travelling together from place to place.

There were also groups who lived together. For example, the community at Qumran, who produced the Dead Sea Scrolls, had a staged entry to the community where members handed over their possessions. The Essenes lived in groups in villages and towns and handed over a proportion of their income each month to the community. Those Jesus calls into relationship with him come from different backgrounds and have different experiences. Here, in Luke 5, he calls both fishermen and a tax collector, and then, in John 4, we see him calling a Samaritan woman. In some cases, those he calls are to leave their existing lives and follow him (Matthew 4:18–22; Mark 1:17–20). For example, in Luke 5:11 the fishermen leave everything to follow Jesus, and later we find them travelling with Jesus (Luke 8:26; 10:38). Others seem to be called to stay where they are (Zacchaeus in Luke 19:1–10; the woman in Simon the Leper's house in Matthew 26:6–13; Martha and Mary in Luke 10:38–42; and Jesus specifically sends the demon-possessed man who has been freed back to his home in Luke 8:38–39).

The group of travelling disciples, some of whom have been called to leave everything, then need a means of support. In John 4, the disciples go into town to buy food, and this may be one of the early stages of the common purse which we will look at in more detail tomorrow. This sharing is not limited to the travelling disciples, as those who are not itinerant are still involved in sharing food or hospitality.

Eating with others was not unusual in the first century any more than it is today. When Levi holds his banquet, Jesus chooses to eat with those who are tax collectors and sinners, in contrast to the expectations of the Pharisees and teachers of the law that someone who was holy would keep himself away from such people (Luke 5:27–30). While Jesus' and his disciples' practice is in some ways specific to their itinerant lifestyle, we can also see patterns and challenges for all followers of Jesus.

2 Betrayal and provisions

Luke 8:1–3; John 12:1–8; 13:21–29

Today's passages include the two times the *glossōkomon* (common purse) is mentioned in the New Testament. While it is only mentioned twice, the references provide some evidence of how the disciples who had left everything to follow Jesus survived, and they point to the way Jesus and his disciples had money that they held together for daily life.

Given that we saw yesterday how some of those Jesus called to follow him were also called to leave their existing way of life, we may wonder where the finance for the common purse came from. Luke 8:1–3 gives us one source of provision. Here we meet three women by the name of Mary, Joanna and Susanna, as well as many others who also travel with Jesus and who help to support him out of their own means. It is also possible that some of the disciples had trades that could be employed as they travelled.

The common purse was used in a number of different ways. As we saw yesterday, it is likely that it was used to buy general provisions for the group (John 4:8) and today's passages indicate this again. When Judas leaves the meal, the disciples think that he may have gone to buy something for the feast (13:29). It is clear from Judas' response to Mary's gift (12:5) and the disciples' expectations when Judas leaves the meal that another of the uses of the common purse was to give to the poor. Despite Judas' pilfering from the common purse (12:6) and his later betrayal of Jesus, the disciples continue to share in this way.

When we look at what we know about Jesus and his disciples and their sharing of possessions, we see that their practice differed from that of other groups, such as the Qumran community and the Essenes. There were different ways of participating as a disciple – some disciples were stationary; others left their possessions and travelled; others took their means with them and travelled. Thus there was more flexibility about how people contributed to the common purse, in comparison to the complete handing over of possessions in the Qumran community and the set proportion of a month's income for those in the Essene communities. Jesus and his disciples also seem to be more open to outsiders than either the Qumran and Essene communities or the Pharisees.

3 Everything in common

Acts 2:37–47

Today's reading includes the first of the summary passages in Acts (vv. 42–47) – a description of the life of those who accepted Peter's message and were baptised (v. 41). It's a picture of a community formed by the work of the Spirit, where sharing possessions is one of the four key characteristics of the fellowship to which the believers continually devoted themselves. This sharing is not a novel activity: as we have seen over the past two sets of readings, Jesus and his disciples shared with one another.

Alongside the apostles' teaching, the breaking of bread and prayer, the believers devote themselves to fellowship (*koinōnia*). *Koinōnia* was also used to indicate generosity, participation and partnership (both in marriage and in business). The summary passage then goes on to explain what this fellowship involves: how they view themselves and their possessions as well as what they do with them. They hold everything in common (v. 44); however, this does not mean that everything is sold and the proceeds placed in one big pot, nor that everything is handed over (as in the Qumran community). Rather, this is how they view what they have, and there is an ongoing process of selling in response to need (v. 45).

In such a situation, those like Mary might continue to own a house which is recognisably hers (12:12), which could also be seen as being held in common in terms of how it is used – for example, as a place for gathering and prayer. The believers also eat together – in fact, in verse 46 the main clause states that they 'ate together with glad and sincere hearts'. Both the meeting in the temple courts and the breaking of bread in homes are dependent on this clause, which suggests that the believers may well be eating together in the temple courts as well as in their homes.

As these early Christians met together and shared their lives and possessions with one another, they saw the Lord growing their community and bringing new believers in.

4 Growth and change

Acts 4:23—5:11

Today's reading includes the second summary passage in Acts (4:32–35) and it takes place in the context of opposition, growth and prayer (4:23–31). Between the first and second summary passages, we see examples of the communal life and faith that are described in both.

In this summary passage, Luke is keen to show how the early community fulfilled both biblical and Graeco-Roman ideals. The phrase 'one in heart and mind' (4:32) picks up on Old Testament passages (Deuteronomy 6:5; 1 Chronicles 12:38) as well as echoing Graeco-Roman literature (Plutarch's *Moralia*, 767E; Cicero's *De Amicitia*, 25.92). The fact that there was no needy person among them (4:34) fulfilled the promise of Deuteronomy 15:4 and was evidence of the presence of God's grace at work in them (4:33).

While there are similarities to the first summary passage, there are also changes. There is no mention of shared meals (maybe in anticipation of the issues of Acts 6:1–6 — was it trickier to eat together in the temple courts? Were they struggling to coordinate the increasing numbers of believers?). In addition, while the ongoing occasional selling continues in response to need, the money is not given directly to those in need, but rather brought to the feet of the apostles and then distributed. This is probably a practical development in a growing fellowship where individuals may struggle to know every member of the wider community and who is in particular need. However, the move could also subvert patronage between wealthier and less well-off believers if the assistance is seen as centrally coordinated. It may also be a way of honouring the apostles.

Luke follows the summary passage with two examples of selling possessions, one positive and one negative. Joseph, also known as Barnabas, sells a field and brings the proceeds to the apostles' feet. We may question why Joseph, as a Levite, had a field, but as the field was in Cyprus it probably fell outside the prohibition of Levites owning land in the promised land. Ananias and Sapphira purport to do the same, but conspire to retain some of the proceeds of the sale while ostensibly laying it all at the feet of the apostles. Peter is clear that the issue is not whether or not they have brought the whole amount, but rather lying to the Holy Spirit, whose presence and actions were so evident in the community.

5 Challenges and complaints

Acts 5:17—6:7

The early church continued to face opposition and persecution with faithfulness and proclamation (5:17–42) and the number of believers continued to grow (6:1, 7). These two factors may be the background causes for the issue between the Hellenist and Hebraic believers. As the community of believers grew in number and faced increasing opposition, they may have found it difficult for everyone to meet or eat together, whether in the temple courts or elsewhere. Spread out in the city, it would have been easy for some of the believers to be overlooked.

The complaint was from those who spoke Greek (maybe they had lived in the diaspora and come to Jerusalem for Pentecost or to die in the city) against those who were Hebrew-speaking – there is not necessarily any difference in how observant of the faith either of the groups were. Some of their widows were being missed in the daily distribution of food. Widows were vulnerable, particularly if they were away from extended family (which, if the Greek-speaking believers had come from the diaspora, they may have been). Later Jewish sources point to two types of provision for those in need: daily provision of food for those who were less well-known in the area (*tamhay*) and weekly provision of money for those who were well-known and in ongoing need (*quppah*). The early church's approach fell between the two, as it involved daily food provision for those who were in ongoing need and who were known to the community. This distribution may have taken place as part of the eating together described in the first summary passage, or may have replaced it if the persecution and growth precluded them eating together in the same way.

The twelve see this complaint as an important issue to resolve, and prioritise it by gathering all the disciples together to find a solution. The twelve do not try to do everything, but rather propose appointing new leaders to this practical task. While it is a practical task, the selection criteria are both spiritual and practical. The seven men chosen all have Greek names, and some of them appear in wider leadership roles as Acts continues (Stephen in chapter 7; Philip in 8:5 and 8:26–40). The growth of the early church points to the need for more leaders. This resolution to the complaint leads to the word of God continuing to spread and increasing numbers of disciples (6:7).

6 Famine and fellowship

Acts 11:19–30

As the persecution of the early church continues, disciples are scattered in the wake of Stephen's death. At the same time, we see the start of the move towards Gentile followers as Cornelius and his family become believers (10:1—11:18). The scattered disciples share the good news as they travel, and in Antioch they share also with Greeks (v. 20), in contrast with those elsewhere who spread the word only among Jews (v. 19).

Barnabas is then sent to Antioch, probably in part to check out what is happening. He rejoices in seeing God at work and fetches Saul to help teach the new believers. During this period Agabus, one of a visiting group of prophets from Jerusalem, predicts a famine. There is plenty of evidence of widespread famine in the 40s and 50s AD. Josephus points to food shortages during the reign of Claudius (*Jewish Antiquities*, 3.320–21) and to Helena and Izates providing relief in Jerusalem (20.51). Tacitus (*Annales*, 12.43), Suetonius (*Divus Claudius*, 18.2) and Pliny (*Natural History*, 5.58; 18.168) all point to food shortages during this period.

The Antiochene believers, each as they are able, contribute to a gift to send. This giving is both an individual decision – each of them gives as they are able – but also a corporate decision – the verb 'decided' is in the plural in the Greek. Given the prediction of famine across the Roman world, we might ask why the gift was designated for the believers in Judea. There was an ongoing link and relationship between the believers in Jerusalem and those in Antioch. It was the scattering of those in Jerusalem that led to the formation of the church in Antioch, and the relationship continued with the sending of Barnabas (v. 22) and the prophets from Jerusalem (v. 27). Thus the Antiochene Christians would have been aware of the specific vulnerabilities of the Jerusalem community (in terms of persecution), but also the wider vulnerabilities of Judea under Roman rule.

The usual Graeco-Roman response to famine was for one or two rich benefactors to subsidise or donate grain in return for honour (for example, a title and/or an inscription in the town). In contrast, the Antiochene Christians involve all the believers, possibly as there were fewer rich people among them who could take on the benefactor role. However, the use of 'disciples' in verse 29 suggests that Luke sees this generous response of giving as a key part of what it means to be a disciple – one who is learning to follow Jesus.

Guidelines

When we look at the common purse and the way Jesus and his disciples shared with one another, we see a number of different ways to contribute and participate. Similarly, in the early church in Acts, we see different ways of being involved and how the believers were free not to give all of the proceeds (but were not free to lie about it).

As the group of disciples grew, there were practical changes in how they shared with one another (bringing proceeds from sales to the disciples' feet rather than directly giving them to the person in need). In addition, both Jesus and his disciples and the early church faced challenges in the practicalities of sharing, both through the actions of individuals and through people being left out due to the ways things were organised (e.g. Judas, Ananias and Sapphira, the Hellenistic widows). For both Jesus and his disciples and the early church, the sharing was part of wider relationships of love, trust and faith.

How do we grow in relationships with our fellow believers when we can share practically with one another?

Where are we already sharing possessions with our brothers and sisters in Christ? How do we need to grow in this?

Does our sharing allow people to contribute and participate in different ways?

Are we ready to grow and change in our sharing in new circumstances and situations?

How do we respond to challenges and issues that arise in our sharing? Do we ignore the issues, do we stop sharing, or do we together tackle the issues?

1 Food and favouritism

1 Corinthians 11:17–34

Today's reading is in some ways more of a 'how not to', as Paul criticises the Corinthians for how they meet together to eat and share the Lord's supper. Paul chastises the Corinthians for the divisions among them, the way some of them go hungry and their shaming of those who have nothing. They do not show the unity they have in Christ or value each person as loved and died for by Christ.

We may wonder what is behind this and why it is happening. Were some believers starting their meals before others? What was going on? Did sharing only happen after the cup of wine was shared after the main meal? The Corinthians were a socially diverse group and they may easily have slipped back into some of the Graeco-Roman traditions and expectations in meal eating. In the ancient world, food was used to distinguish and show honour to particular people. Those with higher status were given special places in the dining room; others may have been crowded in other rooms. Different food and drink was served to guests of different rank. Rather than encouraging equality, meals often reinforced status and hierarchy, and in some cases created it.

In response to the Corinthians' practice, Paul reminds them of Jesus' first sharing of the Lord's supper and self-giving (v. 26). He instructs them to discern the body of Christ (which, in the following chapter, Paul uses to mean the community of believers, though he may use it also to point to Jesus' death and the significance of partaking in the bread), to wait for one another and to examine themselves. This examination is not simply one of moral worthiness, but in relation to one another, so that the way they eat together may proclaim the Lord's death (v. 26). Their behaviour and treatment of one another should be in character with, as opposed to unworthy of (v. 27), the covenant meal they are eating and Jesus' self-giving which established that covenant.

The way they eat together should proclaim the Lord's death and, in so doing, point to the value of each person as part of the body of Christ and the relationship and unity between them.

2 Generosity in poverty

2 Corinthians 8:1–15

In 2 Corinthians 8 and 9, Paul writes to encourage the Corinthians to contribute to the collection for the believers in Jerusalem. Since the initial correspondence about the collection in 1 Corinthians 16:1–4, there have been various ups and downs in his relationship with the Corinthians, and Paul now writes to encourage them to fulfil their initial commitment and desire.

He starts with the example of the Macedonians' giving – a somewhat indirect approach, possibly because of the fragility of his relationship with the Corinthians. The Macedonians gave in the midst of poverty and challenge. There is evidence in the second century BC of mining restrictions leading to economic difficulties in Macedonia. In addition, Acts, 1 Thessalonians and Philippians all report the persecution of believers in the Macedonian region. Despite these challenges, the Macedonians gave voluntarily and with abundant generosity, 'even beyond their ability' (v. 3). Their giving was also first to the Lord and then, out of that, to Paul and the Jerusalem believers. Paul's challenge to the spiritual-gift-focused Corinthians is to excel in this gift and grace of giving (v. 7).

Paul's second example is that of Jesus who, though he was rich, became poor for the sake of the Corinthians (v. 9). The Macedonians gave while they were poor; Jesus gave while he was rich; the Corinthians lie somewhere between the two and are encouraged to follow both of these examples of generosity and giving. Both the Macedonians and Jesus gave voluntarily, and their examples provide a strong encouragement to the Corinthians to give. Paul reassures the Corinthians that his aim is not that they should be in need as a result of their giving but rather that there should be equality (v. 13). He expects that in due course the Corinthians might be on the receiving end of similar giving when they are in need (v. 14). While in Romans 15:25–29 there is a sense of material blessings being given in response to spiritual blessings, here in 2 Corinthians Paul's expectation seems to be of future material reciprocity. To illustrate the kind of equality Paul is thinking about, he uses the example of manna (v. 15; Exodus 16:18). Manna was provided by God; it could not be hoarded and each person ended up with enough. What God effected in the Old Testament, Paul here expects the church to effect.

3 Practical planning

2 Corinthians 8:16—9:5

As well as encouraging the Corinthians to give, Paul also writes to introduce Titus and two other brothers to the Corinthians, who will be involved in organising and transporting the gift. Their visit may also have a wider role to encourage and teach the Corinthians. As with the seven in Acts 6, Titus and the brothers are chosen not simply because of their administrative skills or financial acumen but because of their service to the gospel (8:18, 22) and Christlike character (8:23). They come with significant authority. They have the personal recommendation of Paul. They have been praised by the churches and chosen by them as representatives, and they are 'an honour to Christ' (v. 23). In part, they are appointed out of a concern for financial transparency and honesty.

It is possible that one of the bones of contention between Paul and the Corinthians is financial. Paul had refused help from the Corinthians (probably to avoid being seen as their client) and had offended them by this. Now he is collecting money and it is regarded with suspicion. Titus and the brothers are also to accompany the gift to Jerusalem. As with other first-century methods of transporting money, it was important that people who were trusted (and would not pocket the money) were in charge, but it was also key to have sufficient people accompanying a gift of any size to deter attack from thieves on the potentially slow and arduous journey. Accounts of the way the temple tax was collected in the diaspora show it was carefully transported by groups of people.

In addition to ensuring the probity and security of the gift, it is probable that Titus and the two brothers would have had a teaching role in Corinth during their visit, possibly to continue Paul's teaching on giving. Part of Paul's expressed rationale for the brothers' visit is to avoid any embarrassment of Paul arriving with some Macedonians and discovering that the Corinthians had not fulfilled their earlier eagerness which Paul had reported to the Macedonians.

4 God's generous provision

2 Corinthians 9:6–15

After introducing Titus and the brothers and providing some of the practical details for the transportation of the gift, Paul returns to encouraging the Corinthians to give and provides some theological motivations for giving. He continues to emphasise that giving should be generous (v. 6), voluntary and cheerful (v. 7). He reminds the Corinthians that God is the great provider, who gives and blesses in order to enable us to give – God provides the means for us to give generously. Paul may even have hinted in 2 Corinthians 8:5 that God also provides the desire to give; that through giving themselves first to God, the Macedonians were given the desire to contribute to the gift. In Philippians 2:13, Paul encourages the Philippians that 'it is God who works in you to will and to act in order to fulfil his good purpose'. The gift and service are in themselves part of their confession of the gospel (v. 13) as they live out their obedience to and imitation of Christ.

Paul also points to the way that generous giving supplies the needs of the Lord's people, and results in prayer for the givers and thanks and praise to God. Paul's emphasis on the thanks and praise to God subverts any patronage expectations of the thanks and praise returning to the Corinthians for their gift, and realigns their relationship with those receiving to one that is three-way and centred on Christ. The giving Paul encourages in 2 Corinthians 8—9 is rooted in God and his grace (8:1; 9:8, 14), and in Jesus and his example (8:9); provides for need (8:13–14); is voluntary, generous and practical (8:7–8, 11; 9:5, 8); involves all; is in relation to what people have, though can be sacrificial (8:3, 9, 12); is relational and leads to growing relationships (9:12–15); and has potential reciprocity.

The presence of the brothers also points to the importance of probity, and Paul's final encouragement points to God as the ultimate benefactor, who provides so that the Corinthians may give and thus is the one who will be thanked as a result of the gift.

5 Love and work

1 Thessalonians 4:9–12; 5:12–18

Over the next two days, we will be looking at the issue of the *ataktoi* (idle) in Thessalonica – today at Paul's response in 1 Thessalonians and tomorrow at 2 Thessalonians.

Throughout 1 Thessalonians, Paul's love and affection for the Thessalonians is clear (2:7–8, 11–12, 17). Paul writes to encourage and teach them in the midst of persecution and trials (1:6), and as he does so addresses issues that he has probably heard about from Timothy's recent visit (3:6–7). Paul has already linked love and work in his own life (2:8–9) and, having talked about purity and holiness (4:1–8), now addresses brotherly love and work (4:9–12). Paul praises their love for one another, which he says is God-taught, possibly in contrast to the Epicurean focus on being self-taught. This love is not restricted simply to their brothers and sisters in Thessalonica, but extends to their brothers and sisters throughout Macedonia (maybe evident in their hospitality to others).

Having praised them, Paul goes on to urge them to grow in this love and to make it their political ambition (*philotimeomai*) to live quietly (*hēsuchazeiv*) – a rather odd juxtaposition of words. His exhortation that they should mind their own affairs may well be in contrast to them being concerned with the affairs of a patron (4:11), which would make sense then of the instruction to work with their hands (i.e. to make their living by working, rather than by troubling themselves with the activities of a patron). Paul explains that working rather than being concerned with others' affairs will be a good witness. Being involved in the interests of a patron might provide pressure to compromise their newfound faith if the patron was not also a Christian, as it could include involvement in alternative religious activities. Working will mean that they will not be dependent on anybody. This phrase potentially has both individual and collective meaning.

In 5:14–15, Paul speaks directly about the need to warn the *ataktoi* (idle/disruptive/out of line), but also about helping the weak. Paul's teaching is not simply about the need for believers to work, but rather for encouraging specific believers who are purposefully avoiding work (and maybe relying on patrons) to work. Paul continues in 5:15 to urge the Thessalonians to strive to do good for each other and everyone else. Thus, having spoken against being a client of others, he now encourages the Thessalonians to be benefactors to one another and those outside the community.

6 Limits and doing good

2 Thessalonians 3:6–15

Despite Paul's teaching in 1 Thessalonians, the issue with the *ataktoi* (idle) continued and may even have got worse. We come to Paul's strong response in today's passage.

Why are these people idle and disruptive? What is going on? It is possible that some of them think Jesus' second coming is so close that there is no point in working, or that it is more important to evangelise. However, while Paul addresses eschatology in both letters, he does not link it to the issue about work and idleness. Also, in using eschatological language, Paul may be contrasting Jesus with the emperor, who was also spoken about with such language.

Another possibility is the one we looked at yesterday, that patronage expectations may be behind the issue of some people not working – maybe because they think they are now free in Christ and above manual work. Others may have been clients of non-Christian patrons and found difficulties once they became Christians with some of their expectations, therefore looking to richer Christians to act as their patrons instead.

Whatever the precise causes, some of the Thessalonians are refusing to work, expecting others to support them and being disruptive. In response, Paul gives them the model of how he acted among them for them to follow: how he worked hard and was not a burden (vv. 7–8). It is important to remember here that Paul has also been very clear about helping those who were weak (1 Thessalonians 5:14) and is here speaking to those who are habitually refusing to work rather than those who cannot work.

Paul reminds the Thessalonians of what he had laid down when he was with them: 'The one who is unwilling to work shall not eat' (v. 10). In Greek, this is an imperative: 'let them not eat'. This indicates that the Thessalonians were eating together sufficiently often to be able to withhold food from those who were idle. It is here that we see more clearly that the *ataktoi* were not simply idle or refusing to work; they were also disruptive and busybodies (v. 11).

Paul goes on to exhort the whole congregation to never tire of doing what is good – *kalopoiéō* (v. 13), using a word that could point to patronage and benefaction. In other words, Paul is calling the Thessalonians to be benefactors rather than to look for one or two of their members to be the patrons for others.

Guidelines

The Corinthian church was a diverse community that Paul was encouraging to behave in countercultural ways – in how they ate together, but also in how they gave. Paul sent Titus and the brothers to help with the practical organisation of the gift – to ensure both financial probity and security. Paul also reminded the Corinthians of God's character and generosity towards them, providing for them (and us) to be generous givers without patronage expectations.

With the Thessalonians, Paul was quick to praise their love and care for one another, but also placed boundaries on this sharing, encouraging the Thessalonians who were able to work to do so rather than being concerned with the affairs of a patron and seeking to rely on them.

As we look at the Corinthians and the Thessalonians, what can we learn? When do we share food with one another?

How do we relate to and share with those brothers and sisters who are different from us? In our Christian communities, how do we make sure everyone is included and no one is left out?

Are we ready to give and receive in sharing? Which do we find easiest?

What do we put in place to guard probity? How do we value and learn from those with gifts in the areas of finance and administration?

Paul encouraged both the Corinthians and the Thessalonians to give without patronage expectations. Are we ready to freely give as we have freely received?

Paul encouraged all the Corinthians to take part in the gift (voluntarily) and all the Thessalonians to behave as benefactors to those around them. How do we hold the tension between encouraging participation in giving and making clear that it is voluntary?

In what ways are Christians currently benefactors to those around them?

FURTHER READING

Craig L. Blomberg, *Neither Poverty nor Riches* (Apollos, 1999).

Fiona J.R. Gregson, *Everything in Common? The theology and practice of the sharing of possessions in community in the New Testament* (Pickwick Publications, 2017).

Luke Timothy Johnson, *Sharing Possessions* (SCM, 1981).

Trevor J. Saxby, *Pilgrims of a Common Life: Christian community of goods through the centuries* (Herald, 1987).

Ben Witherington, *Jesus and Money* (SPCK, 2010).

The spirituality of the prophets

Paul Hedley Jones

The Old Testament does not hold back from depicting the tension between God's good intentions and human resistance. But wherever the balance is strained between human decision and divine intention, prophetic intervention is never far afield. Throughout scripture, the prophets show up at every critical juncture, seeking to pull the people of God back in line with his intentions for them. Simply put, Israel's prophets are men and women who share God's passion. And as Yahweh's passions are inscribed upon the prophets, they become instruments in his hands, through whom he breathes divine sentiments of grief (1 Samuel 15:11), jealousy (Exodus 34:14), rejoicing (Isaiah 62:5), love (Hosea 3:1) and so on. In many respects, Israel's prophets are precursors to Jesus of Nazareth, whose prophetic ministry brings about the fulfilment of God's passion to dwell on earth among his people.

So if we want to know what it looks like for a human life to share God's passion, we can do no better than to turn to the prophets. While they may not embody God's perfect self-revelation as Jesus does, the prophets are certainly on the same continuum as visible, personal manifestations of God to his defiant partner Israel.

The following twelve studies, drawn from the author's book *Sharing God's Passion* (Paternoster, 2012), offer snapshots of prophetic spirituality by focusing on events in the lives of six men and women (Moses, Deborah, Samuel, Elijah, Jeremiah and Jonah) who were called to don the prophetic mantle.

Quotations are from the New International Version (Anglicised).

1 Israel's prophetic vocation

Exodus 20:18–26

If we define prophecy as 'human speech on behalf of God', God's decision to entrust Israel with his 'ten words' (the commandments) was tantamount to a prophetic calling on a national level. On Mount Sinai, God entrusted his words to Israel and then asked her to behave in ways that would 'speak' those words to the rest of the world: 'Be holy, because I am holy.' This raises an interesting question: if Yahweh entrusted the entire nation with the prophetic task of being his ambassadors in the world, why did prophets exist within Israel as individuals?

Many Christians know Exodus 20 to be a chapter in the Old Testament that contains the ten commandments (also Deuteronomy 5). But all too often, we stop reading after the tenth commandment and miss what happens next. Verses 18–26 suggest that a primary reason Israel had individual prophets was the nation's fear of drawing too near to God. Upon receiving the commandments at Mount Sinai, the terrified Israelites ask Moses to become their go-between. 'When the people saw the thunder and lightning and heard the trumpet and saw the mountain in smoke, they trembled with fear. They stayed at a distance and said to Moses, "Speak to us yourself and we will listen. But do not have God speak to us or we will die"' (vv. 18–19; see also Deuteronomy 5:22–31). Israel's request, which God approves, is followed by a summary statement in verse 21 that captures the essence of Moses' prophetic call: 'The people remained at a distance, while Moses approached the thick darkness where God was.' Israel's response to the theophany explains how one man came to bear the weight of God's words to Israel.

In spite of this, Israel's prophetic role in Yahweh's purposes is a theme that continues to expand throughout the Old Testament, notably in the preaching of the prophets. It is hardly surprising that Isaiah's portraits of the suffering servant combine the office of a prophet, the nation of Israel and a messianic figure into a single personification. For, as we shall see, Israel's calling to bless the nations through obedience to the covenant was preached most rigorously by her prophets and ultimately fulfilled by her representative Messiah. In what ways might your words and actions today reflect the prophetic vocation of all God's people?

2 'I wish all the Lord's people were prophets!'

Numbers 11:10–17, 24–30

Only days after leaving Sinai (and a year since leaving Egypt), with the leadership of God's people squarely upon his shoulders, Moses came close to collapsing under the weight of Israel's whining. In his distress, he hurled a series of questions at Yahweh, begging for intervention and even confessing that he would prefer to be smitten by God than to face his own ruin at the hands of the Israelites. In response, God proposed to disperse his Spirit upon 70 selected elders to alleviate the pressure on Moses. As Yahweh's Spirit came upon the elders gathered at the tent of meeting, they began to prophesy, although we are not told exactly what they said or did. The narrative is more interested in Joshua's reaction to two elders who were evidently in the wrong place at the right time and who had begun prophesying in the camp rather than in the tent of meeting.

This was the first time since Israel received the commandments that anyone besides Moses had prophesied, and since the responsibility for speaking God's words had hitherto fallen solely to Moses, it is not surprising that Joshua responded as he did: 'Moses, my lord, stop them!' (v. 28).

Joshua's efforts to protect the prophetic office from unauthorised use were understandable, but Moses was neither alarmed nor offended by what had happened. On the contrary, he responded with crystal clarity – and with some exasperation, no doubt: 'Are you jealous for my sake? I wish all the Lord's people were prophets and that the Lord would put his Spirit on them!' (v. 29).

Moses' first concern, far from claiming exclusive prophetic rights for those gathered at the tent of meeting, was that 70 prophets would not be enough. It would appear from his response that not being in the 'right' place geographically (i.e. the tent of meeting) was not a problem in Moses' mind. Nor was it an issue for Yahweh, who obviously deemed the two men worthy of his Spirit regardless of their location.

A second implication for our study of prophetic spirituality is Moses' expressed desire that the Israelites were capable of fulfilling their prophetic vocation without him having to function as the middleman. Some scholars observe that Moses' wish is finally fulfilled at Pentecost (Acts 2), where twelve Spirit-filled apostles demonstrate that sharing God's passion is still the prophetic task of his people.

3 Collaborating with God

The book of Judges has been described as cyclical, or perhaps more accurately as a downward spiral: Israel sins; Israel is oppressed; Israel cries out; God delivers. Rinse and repeat.

What is new and surprising in each cycle is the raising up of a new deliverer. In Judges 4, we are introduced to Deborah, who is characterised by just two qualities: as a prophetess, she speaks on God's behalf (v. 4); as a judge, she settles the disputes of the people (v. 5). As the narrative unfolds and these qualities are fleshed out, it becomes clear that her ability to close the gap between human and divine activity is the key to breaking Israel's cycle of sin.

As someone attuned to what God is doing in and through Israel, Deborah summons Israel's military general – Barak – into action. The chapter then tells of the respective victories of Barak (vv. 6–15) and Jael (vv. 17–24). A key thing to notice in these tales is that each sub-story highlights the important role played by God's human partners in the fulfilment of his purposes. Divine intention and human decision are drawn together by Deborah's prophetic wisdom to ensure certain victory.

Barak's victory concludes with this summary statement: 'At Barak's advance, the Lord routed Sisera and all his chariots and army by the sword, and Sisera got down from his chariot and fled on foot' (v. 15). Notice that the Lord is credited with routing Sisera, even as the narrator states that this was accomplished 'by the sword' – that is, the swords of Israel.

Similarly, in the story of Jael, the narrator concludes with a dual recognition of both God and Israel: 'On that day God subdued Jabin king of Canaan before the Israelites. And the hand of the Israelites pressed harder and harder against Jabin king of Canaan until they destroyed him' (vv. 23–24). 'God subdued Jabin', but the Israelites 'destroyed him'. In this story of divine–human cooperation, the author accentuates the collaborative success of God together with his people. Yes, Deborah exemplifies Yahweh's working relationship with his prophets, but hers are not the only actions that matter.

Monotonous cycles of sin, no matter how small, are an early symptom of the malaise of indifference, a sign that we have begun to lose sight of God's big picture. Deborah's story is a powerful reminder that when we are wise enough to share God's vision for his world and courageous enough to collaborate with him, a spark of initiative can break cycles of sin that bind and oppress.

4 'Help the Lord against the mighty'

Judges 5

Judges 5 presents a poetic reprise to reinforce the accent of the preceding prose account. The song of Deborah commemorates and celebrates the interplay of Yahweh's decisive acts and the willing cooperation of the prophetess. Human leadership is juxtaposed with a divine hero.

Notice how, in verses 1–7, the songwriter oscillates between the actions of Deborah and the praise of Yahweh, with glory being ascribed both to God as Lord of creation and to Deborah and other human agents who have taken initiative on the ground. In verse 11, the point is wonderfully made by placing 'the victories of the Lord' in parallel with 'the victories of his villagers in Israel'. But the songwriter goes on to make the same point with even greater force.

Having paid tribute to the tribes of Israel that came willingly to Yahweh's aid (vv. 14–15a, 18), the song then condemns the reluctance of those tribes that failed to participate in God's initiatives (vv. 15b–17). In a surprising turn of phrase, the people of Meroz are cursed 'because they did not come to help the Lord, to help the Lord against the mighty' (v. 23).

If it seems strange or wrong to speak of *helping* God, it is only because of our tendency to think of God as the only one who makes things happen. The point, of course, is not that God is helpless without us; we would be in dire straits if that were so! But, for better or worse, God has chosen for it to be this way. It is vital that the church today resists an attitude that abandons God to do 'his work', and that we seek rather to understand the pivotal role we are invited to play in renewing the world.

To really hammer the point home (if you'll excuse the pun), the songwriter concludes by juxtaposing a blessing for Jael with a curse on those who refuse to cooperate with God. Even Jael, a non-Israelite, served as God's instrument of victory because of her swift initiatives in the heat of the moment (vv. 24–27). God may not *need* human assistance, but the Old Testament repeatedly makes it clear that he desires our cooperation and happily blesses those who choose to help him.

5 An ethic of confrontation

1 Samuel 3

This chapter does not begin on a very hopeful note: 'In those days the word of the Lord was rare.' The scarcity of God's word was most likely a consequence of Israel's disobedience. (More than 200 years later, the prophet Amos would threaten to withdraw Yahweh's word from a people who paid it no heed: Amos 8:11–12.) These were dark times, as indicated by the themes of light and sight in the opening verses (1 Samuel 3:1–3).

As priest, Eli was responsible for sustaining purity in Israel. But his sons, Hophni and Phinehas, were treating the sacrifices of the people with contempt and even sleeping with the female servants at the tent of meeting which Moses had established as a place to meet with God. Rather than preserving purity in Israel, these men were perverting the priesthood and leading Israelites into sin.

Enter Samuel, a young prophet called by a God whose voice he does not yet recognise (v. 7), despite the fact that he serves in Yahweh's temple. (Note that this is an indictment of Eli, not young Samuel.) The story of Samuel's thrice-repeated 'Here I am' as he confuses Yahweh's voice with Eli's is a familiar one for its portrayal of childlike innocence in responding to God's call. But the story doesn't end with Samuel's recognition of the voice of God; it goes on to introduce a core attribute of Israel's prophets: an ethic of confrontation.

Having been introduced to Yahweh during the night, Samuel awakens with the knowledge that he must bring down the man who has brought him up. At Eli's bidding, the young prophet faithfully delivers a word of severe judgement, a word which Eli appears to accept quite readily, perhaps because he has already heard it once before (1 Samuel 2:30).

The chapter concludes with the report of Samuel's reputation spreading like wildfire. This is a prophet of Yahweh whose words never fall to the ground (v. 19), which is to say that they never fail to accomplish the purpose for which they are sent (Isaiah 55:11; 1 Kings 2:27). And, as Samuel matures, verbal assaults on compromise continue to characterise his prophetic ministry. After this first confrontation with Israel's priesthood, Samuel goes on to confront the people (1 Samuel 8; 12) and their king (1 Samuel 15; 28) in his efforts to draw Israel into line with God's purposes.

6 Heart reorientation

1 Samuel 8:1–8; 15:10–23

Samuel's repeated experiences of prophetic conflict expose deep problems within Israel and the nation's leadership. In each case, however, the sinful behaviour addressed is only the symptom of a deeper 'heart problem'.

Eli is punished because 'his sons uttered blasphemies against God, and he failed to restrain them' (1 Samuel 3:13). Blasphemy, the profaning of God's name, is something more than just saying the wrong kinds of words when you feel frustrated. Rather, it refers to the misrepresentation of God's character that ends up giving him a bad name; in other words, saying you represent God ('taking God's name…') but not acting like it ('…in vain'). It is the hottest topic in the preaching of the prophets.

To the people in 1 Samuel 8, Samuel points out that their sin lies in their request to 'be like all the other nations' (v. 20). The very purpose of Israel's distinct identity was to make God known by being unlike the surrounding nations, so their request for a human king was not just a matter of Israel coveting what others had, but one of trading in her divine calling.

In 1 Samuel 15, Saul clearly fails to recognise that Israel's human king must remain subservient to her true King. Saul bent rules and commands to suit his royal self, and as a result the crown passed to David, whose heart was a more accurate reflection of Yahweh's heart (1 Samuel 13:14).

Do you see the pattern? Eli's sons misrepresented God by doing awful things in his name; Israel misrepresented God by wanting to be like everybody else; and Saul misrepresented God by making up his own rules as Yahweh's representative. In each case, beneath the distinct acts of disobedience and rebellion was a wayward heart needing reorientation so that God's covenant people might properly present his character to the nations.

By the same token, the goal of Christian ethics is not simply to 'be good' so that we are less plagued by guilt on our journey through life. The problem with that kind of tunnel vision is that we become obsessed with our own personal war against sin, which then becomes the primary means of measuring success or failure. Like all of Israel's prophets, Samuel longed to see God's people reflecting God's likeness while the rest of the world looked on. But his confrontational ethic sought to establish not just obedience, but obedience *as a means of speaking for God*.

Guidelines

This week, with Moses, Deborah and Samuel, we have already seen that God's good intention for people to enflesh his image upon the earth is especially evident in the lives of his prophets. Indeed, the prophets demand our attention if we would stand with them to bridge the gap between God's relentless love for the world and the human propensity to sin (see Ezekiel 22:30). In the coming week, we consider how we may learn from the narrative world of scripture in order to live our own lives differently. Reciting ancient stories in today's language or melting complex tales down into so-called timeless truths may serve a purpose, but if we wish to experience biblical narratives in some way, we must be prepared to fill the gaps left by the narrator – both on and off the page.

In the coming week, as we read stories of Elijah, Jeremiah and Jonah, I encourage you to put yourself in their shoes and ask how you might represent God in your own particular context, in both word and speech. When we enter the storied world of scripture, new possibilities arise through the intersection of the textual world (on the page) with our world (off the page). What's more, as we enter the world of scripture, the biblical stories penetrate the crusted surface of our lives and enter our thinking, changing the way we perceive God, our neighbours, our planet and ourselves. In this way, these sacred stories expose us (far more than stale routines or weighty rules) to profound opportunities for transformation, as the Spirit of the word leads us.

1 You are what you worship

1 Kings 18:1–21

Idolatry is depicted as the greatest threat to God's people in the Old Testament, and it is a theme addressed by the prophets countless times. The first two commandments given to Israel at Sinai prohibit the worship of false gods and the creation of idols (Exodus 20:3–6), but false worship is not simply wrong because God is a jealous God. A theological principle running through the Old Testament, and undergirding the prohibition of false worship, is that humans come to resemble that which they worship. In other words, idolatry is abhorrent to the Creator because it distorts the images of God (i.e. human beings) that he created to represent him. The first two commandments affirm these twin truths: there is only one true God, and only one appropriate image for God on earth: human beings.

Accordingly, Isaiah proclaims, in Isaiah 48:4, that when Israel worships idols made of iron and bronze, the nation develops an iron neck (stubbornness) and a bronze forehead (a dull mind). Jeremiah also warns the people of Judah, saying, 'Do not follow other gods to your own harm' (Jeremiah 7:6), because he understands that idolatry dehumanises them. Since human beings were made to reflect God's image, the worship of anything else desecrates what God has entrusted to us, whether that damage be psychological, emotional or even physical, as we will see in the story of Elijah on Mount Carmel (see also Psalm 115:4–8).

It is perhaps understandable, in a world of such swift and uncertain change as ours, why people grope optimistically at false idols that promise security through wealth, popularity, sex and power. But if the psalmists and prophets are right, trusting in impersonal, senseless things only makes people less personal and less sensible – in other words, less like the God whose image we were created to reflect.

Israel's idolatry is presented in 1 Kings 18 as having dangerous and damaging consequences. Ahab fails to grasp that Elijah's three-year weather forecast reflects the nation's dried-up spiritual condition (1 Kings 17:1). And when Elijah goes before the people to rebuke them for their mixed loyalties, he asks, 'How long will you waver [*or* limp] between two opinions? If the Lord is God, follow him; but if Baal is God, follow him.' The wording is suggestive of Israel's spiritually crippled condition. And significantly, like the speechless god they worship, the people say nothing. They are mute. You are what you worship.

2 Idolatry as self-harm

1 Kings 18:22–40

The rules of the contest are straightforward: two altars are set up, bearing sacrifices to be set alight by a deity in response to the pleas of representative prophets. Baal versus Yahweh. Only a demonstration of genuine power – fire from heaven – would prove one god's superiority over the other. And so the contest begins, with the prophets of Baal going first and Elijah taunting them from morning until evening.

To press his theological point, the writer uses the same word in verse 26 that was used by Elijah (v. 21) to describe Baal's prophets as they 'limp' around their altar with no response from their god. God's people limp in compromise just as the prophets of Baal limp in their misguided worship. Moreover, as the prophets of Baal begin slashing themselves with swords and spears in desperation, the story reinforces the principle that idolatry is divisive and dehumanising (see Jeremiah 7:18–19). Trying to have it both ways does more harm than good.

There is only one true God, shouts the prophet. If it is Yahweh, follow him! If Baal, then seek him! But stop limping about with a foot in both camps! A similar mandate would be uttered centuries later to the Christian church in Laodicea: 'I know your deeds, that you are neither cold nor hot. I wish you were either one or the other! So, because you are lukewarm – neither hot nor cold – I am about to spit you out of my mouth' (Revelation 3:15–16).

And so the entire day passes with Baal's prophets shouting and screaming, praying and prophesying, and cutting themselves to shreds. Elijah taunts his rivals all day by stressing Baal's absence, until finally the narrator affirms the same reality: 'There was no response, no one answered, no one paid attention' (v. 29). Silence. Nothing. No one.

In accordance with Isaiah's preaching (Isaiah 41:21–24), false gods are deaf, mute and powerless. Baal is evidently as harmless as 'a scarecrow in a cucumber field' (Jeremiah 10:5), although it is not just Baal who is lost in deathly silence. The people of Israel offering him (half) their allegiance are equally silent and King Ahab is also conspicuously absent from the whole affair. Again, the silence of Baal is reflected in the muteness of his subjects. You are what you worship.

3 Malleable clay

Jeremiah 18:1–11

Jeremiah was immensely unpopular in Jerusalem for his doom-and-gloom sermons. But in spite of his desolate tone, Jeremiah also affirmed that things *could* be different. Indeed, Jeremiah 18 contains a revelation of crystal clarity regarding the profound impact human decisions can have upon God's actions in the world.

Arriving at the potter's house in response to Yahweh's instruction, Jeremiah watches carefully as the artisan goes about his work. The first thing he notices, other than the use of a pottery wheel, is that the potter begins his work with a particular goal in mind. However, if a vessel loses its intended shape and becomes corrupted somehow, then the clay is reworked and an alternative outcome is chosen for it (v. 4). As Jeremiah stands by, observing the craftsman's movements, a word from Yahweh comes to him as promised: 'Can I not do with you, Israel, as this potter does?... Like clay in the hand of the potter, so are you in my hand, Israel' (v. 6).

On first impressions, the metaphor appears to put everything in God's hands with little left to human responsibility. But the presence of a potter's wheel suggests that Israel is not simply inert matter, for when clay is spinning on a wheel, it generates a force of its own. In fact, as Yahweh goes on to explain the significance of the metaphor, this is precisely the point he makes: even when God has foretold his intentions through a prophet, Israel's response to that prophetic word is taken seriously enough for God to genuinely reconsider and modify his proposed course of action.

Jeremiah's brief excursion down handicrafts lane reinforces the Potter's sovereignty without undermining the innate potential of the clay. The staggering truth is that God's decisions regarding the future, revealed through his messengers, are generally contingent upon human attitudes and actions in the present (see also Ezekiel 33:11–20). While prophetic speech often resounds with certainty, it is actually conditional in many cases because God takes human behaviour so seriously. In spite of Jeremiah's tendency to preach sermons of woe, Judah's future – like that of malleable clay – is still very much open, either for ruin or restoration.

4 A broken jar

Jeremiah 19:1–15

In this chapter, Jeremiah is instructed a second time to go to a potter's house, this time to buy an already-fashioned (hardened) pot. The metaphor of God's people as clay in his hands is present again, but where the metaphor in chapter 18 emphasised Israel's part in co-determining the future, the enacted parable of Jeremiah 19 announces that God is going to change Jerusalem for ever: 'This is what the Lord Almighty says: I will smash this nation and this city just as this potter's jar is smashed and cannot be repaired' (v. 11).

God and his messenger have been rejected and Judah has chosen her path. She is as stubborn (Jeremiah 18:12) and stiff-necked (19:15) as her sister Israel, and the image of clay is therefore altered to match her hardened resolve.

Our lives follow a similar pattern, do they not? As long as we are responsive to the nudging of God's Spirit, we remain pliable in his hands, but when repeated acts of rebellion numb and harden us, we eventually find ourselves immobilised by pride. Sometimes only a crisis can break us and wake us to be refashioned in God's image. The language of Jeremiah 18—19 provides us with two powerful symbols for reflection.

What course is your life taking due to the condition of your heart? Are you closed off to future possibilities because you have become overly rigid in certain ways? Are you being moulded in the Potter's hands according to his will, or must you be broken to begin afresh?

Tragically, in Jeremiah 19, Jeremiah takes the purchased pot to Potsherd Gate in obedience to God's instruction, where he proceeds to smash it and prophesy against Jerusalem as instructed. Since no appropriate response is made by the people, God acts in history as he said he would and Judah receives her judgement.

But there is another side to Judah's tragic demise, since these chapters also reflect the suffering of God and his spokesman (Jeremiah 18:13–23). In short, God loves the world to the point of suffering, and the lives of prophets such as Jeremiah point us forward to the incarnation, where the shared suffering of another prophet and his God take the shape of the cross for the sake of the world.

5 Digesting the word

Jonah 4:1–5

Prophets were required to ingest God's mandate fully into their own lives before proclaiming it to others. A vivid image for this principle in scripture is the consumption of a scroll. See, as examples, Ezekiel 3:1–4, Jeremiah 15:16 and Revelation 10:10–11. The pattern is relatively simple – eat the scroll and deliver God's word – but the action suggests not just a command to practise what is preached, but something far more profound: God's word taking on flesh.

Sadly, in Jonah's case, the notion of digesting God's word is turned on its head (or tail?) when the messenger rather than the message becomes the thing swallowed. Fortunately for Jonah, the great fish finds him as unpalatable as Jonah finds God's merciful word. In the final chapter of this small book, readers learn that God's mercy is the very reason for Jonah's disobedience to his prophetic commission!

Isn't this what I said, Lord, when I was still at home? That is what I tried to forestall by fleeing to Tarshish. I knew that you are a gracious and compassionate God, slow to anger and abounding in love, a God who relents from sending calamity.

JONAH 4:2

To this defiant prophet, God's mercy is displeasing because it is far too accessible, reaching even to the Assyrians. (The Assyrians were responsible for the conquer and exile of Israel in 722BC.) But in the same breath, Jonah reveals that he also knows Israel's creed concerning Yahweh's character (see Exodus 34:6; Joel 2:13–14). The critical issue here is that Jonah knows this word about God, but he has not digested it. He simply cannot bring himself to accept that Yahweh may wish to extend his mercy beyond Israel's borders. And although his five-word sermon has the kind of radical impact on Nineveh that would make any preacher jealous, God's merciful response is not what Jonah was hoping for. On the contrary, he is so far from sharing God's passion that the characteristic mercy of God is something he considers a great evil (Jonah 4:1)!

Why is this so? Tragically, Jonah cannot stomach the bittersweet message of mercy that is rooted in forgiven-ness and subsequently expressed in forgiveness. Our capacity to show mercy to others is a fruit that grows in proportion to our own acceptance of God's mercy; as Jesus taught, the two are inseparable (see Matthew 6:14–15).

6 A right to be angry?

Jonah 4:6–11

As the dust settles from Jonah's outburst against divine mercy, God again exercises his power over creation to teach Jonah a lesson. A vine provides Jonah with shade to ease his discomfort, which has (somewhat ironically) been caused by God's mercy (v. 6). But no sooner does Jonah begin to cheer up than a worm is sent to kill the vine. Without its shade, Jonah is burnt by the sun and scorched by a wind from the desert. For the second time comes God's question: 'Do you have a right to be angry?' to which Jonah responds, 'I am angry enough to die!' (v. 9).

To help Jonah understand things from the divine perspective, God gives him a plant to shade him – something the prophet takes great pleasure in – and then takes it away again. Jonah is set up to feel a sense of loss over the vine so that he may even *slightly* begin to identify with God's concern for 120,000 spiritually disoriented Ninevites 'who cannot tell their right hand from their left' (v. 11). But, rather than coming to any neat conclusions, the book of Jonah ends with a question (vv. 10–11). Of course, if Jonah were worth his salt as a prophet, such a question would not need to be asked at all. But the literary artistry of the book leaves the question to resonate in the ears of its readers as well. Biblical narratives invite readers *in* so that we may live *out* our responses to the text. We cannot know whether Jonah repented or remained angry, but readers can give the story closure by making their own response to it.

Attitudes of exclusion often grow out of a notion of purity that sees anything different or 'other' to be dangerous, a potential threat to our (imagined) purity. At their worst, perverse notions like this lead to heinous crimes against humanity, acts of exclusion as horrific as the Holocaust or the Rwandan genocide of 1994, but the seeds for such acts of exclusion are certainly closer to home. Sometimes even deeds of apparent righteousness, designed to separate and protect us from 'the world' become exclusionary if we end up distancing ourselves from the very people Jesus came to love, to heal and to save (see Mark 2:17).

Guidelines

These biblical narratives about the prophets don't say everything. They leave gaps to be filled by the reader's imagination. Gap-filling is one of the keys to successful storytelling, scriptwriting and, for that matter, preaching. Unlike novels and films, however, an appropriate response to scripture requires more than just a mental response, since 'faith by itself, if it is not accompanied by action, is dead' (James 2:17).

When the Bible presents us with a question, it is almost always more than a riddle requiring a brainy solution. In fact, the Bible's tough questions and challenges cannot be solved in the pulpit at all. Rather, they must be answered in our living, by the decisions we make from Sunday to Saturday. If, upon reading about Elijah upon Mount Carmel (1 Kings 18), readers find themselves convicted of 'limping between two opinions' and are prompted to join Israel in putting false gods aside, then an appropriate interpretation of the text will include an act of repentance. False gods will be put aside in response to a word that seeks to engage our whole lives. Gap-filling, for Bible readers, is much more than an intellectual exercise, for we seek not only the renewing of our minds, but also fresh opportunities to offer ourselves as living sacrifices before a God who awaits our answer (1 Kings 18:39; Romans 12:1–2).

The point is not that interpretation and transformation are of equal importance, but rather that our embodied response to God's word *is* the most meaningful interpretive act. One result of our endeavours to express the meanings of biblical narratives in this way is that their plots remain intertwined with our own life stories, even after the Bible is back on the bookshelf or bedside table.

FURTHER READING

Terence Fretheim, *The Suffering of God: An Old Testament perspective* (Fortress, 1984).

Abraham Joshua Heschel, *The Prophets* (Harper, 1969).

Paul Hedley Jones, *Sharing God's Passion: Prophetic spirituality* (Paternoster, 2012).

Nahum

Miriam Hinksman

The book of Nahum is an oracle against Nineveh, infamous capital city of Assyria – the universally hated superpower in the ancient Near East at the time. The northern kingdom of Israel had fallen to Assyria in 722BC, and Judah had been dominated by them ever since, about 100 years by the time Nahum's prophecy appears. Nahum dates between the fall of Thebes in 663BC (referenced in Nahum 3) and 612BC, when Nineveh was overthrown by the Babylonians. Nahum's announcement of judgement on Nineveh is both an implicit and explicit message of salvation for Judah.

Nahum contrasts starkly with the book of Jonah, which also famously contains an oracle against Nineveh. In Jonah, the oracle is brief and to the point ('Forty days more, and Nineveh shall be overthrown!', Jonah 3:4). It is also effective, prompting repentance among the Ninevites and a change of heart on Yahweh's part, who decides not to destroy the city after all. There is no such repenting and relenting in Nahum. Rather, there is startling and confronting imagery throughout, as Nahum's vivid and powerful poetry brutally portrays Nineveh's coming devastation. It is probably as well we have both reports of Yahweh's accounting with the same enemy nation in scripture.

It is difficult to discern a clear structure for the book of Nahum, and the Hebrew text is also difficult in places. But there is certainly unity of theme and message: Yahweh is God of all nations and will utterly destroy his enemies. While Assyria in God's hand was a powerful rod for chastising his own people, there comes a point when God says, enough is enough. Assyria has gone too far and become God's enemy. And Nahum is unequivocal: you really, really don't want to be an enemy of this God.

Unless otherwise stated, quotations are from the New Revised Standard Version.

1 Concerning Nineveh, comforting Judah

Nahum 1:1–8

The book of Nahum declares its interest from the outset as 'an oracle concerning Nineveh' (v. 1). The prophet Nahum is identified only by a place, Elkosh. Nahum is unknown elsewhere in the Bible, and the location of Elkosh is only known conjecturally. The name Nahum may therefore be symbolic rather than identifying an actual person. Nahum means 'comfort' (compare with Nehemiah, 'comfort of the Lord') and as such the vision can be understood as a message of comfort to Judah (compare Isaiah 40:1), despite large portions being addressed to Nineveh itself.

This comfort consists in the first instance of the assurance that God is 'a jealous and avenging God', who is 'avenging and wrathful' and 'takes vengeance on his adversaries' (v. 2) – in this case, Nineveh. For Judeans who had been subject to Assyria's domination for nigh on 100 years, saying, 'The Lord is slow to anger' (v. 3) must have seemed like an understatement. Now Judah is assured that, while slow to anger, Yahweh has in fact noticed the Assyrians' cruelty, his wrath burns against them and they will 'by no means' be cleared of their crimes (v. 3).

Verses 2–8 form a partial acrostic, with successive lines more or less beginning with the first eleven letters of the Hebrew alphabet. This is also a theophany, the appearance of God made manifest through physical demonstrations of power in the natural world: whirlwind and storm (v. 3); clouds and dust (v. 3); seas drying up (v. 4); famously fertile regions withering away (v. 4); mountains shaking (v. 5); hills melting (v. 5); earth heaving (v. 5); fire (v. 6); rocks breaking (v. 6); and an overwhelming flood (v. 8). This imagery demonstrates God's sovereignty over the whole earth (compare Psalm 8) – and all the nations thereof – and thus when Nahum announces that God will make a 'full end' of Nineveh (v. 8) there is no doubt that he can and will do what he says.

Within this hymn emphasising God's power and wrath comes a nugget of hope for Judah: those who trust in the Lord find him to be 'good,' a 'stronghold in a day of trouble' (v. 7). I know whose side I want to be on in the day God 'pursue[s] his enemies into darkness' (v. 8)!

2 The end is coming

Verse 9 asks anyone who would plot against Yahweh what on earth they think they're doing. Plots against Yahweh can only come to nothing, as it is re-emphasised that he will make a 'full end' of any adversary (compare v. 8). Three images of those who plot against Yahweh follow: they are like tangled thorns, drunks and stubble consumed by a fire (v. 10). These images may seem unrelated in English, but in Hebrew they are linked by the assonance of the 's' sounds of the letters *samech* and *sin*.

The alternation of announcements of judgement and salvation in verses 11–15 makes it difficult to determine to whom these verses are addressed, especially when the gender of each addressee and whether they are plural or singular is lost in translation. Various translations attempt to clarify the ambiguity, with the NIV determining that the recipient of the judgements in verses 11 and 14 is Nineveh, while the addressee whose affliction is ended in verse 12 is Judah (compare v. 15). This would certainly fit with the overall message of Nahum as one of comfort to Judah and destruction for Nineveh.

In verse 11, the address is in the second-person feminine singular, which could indicate its direction to the city of Nineveh or Jerusalem. Cities were often referred to in feminine terms in the ancient world. The NIV inserts 'Nineveh', probably correctly surmising that the city from whom the evil plotter and worthless counsellor went out was Assyria's capital. The idea that plotting evil against Yahweh is futile is continued in verse 12: 'They will be cut off and pass away.'

There follows a complete reversal in tone. In another second-person feminine singular address, someone is promised that their affliction is ended, and that the yoke and bonds (of slavery as a vassal state) will be broken. The NIV surmises that the address is now to Judah, inserting 'Judah' in translation. It should be noted, though, that these clarifications are not present in the Hebrew, and the NRSV, for example, allows the ambiguity to remain.

In another about-turn, verse 14 pronounces judgement again. This address is in the second-person masculine singular, and thus is probably directed at the king of Assyria (compare 3:18–19).

Finally, verse 15 turns again to 'good tidings', this time making clear in the Hebrew text that it is Judah who is promised a proclamation of peace.

3 Devastation, desolation, destruction

These verses graphically depict Nineveh's fall. They start by calling the city and its inhabitants to defend the fortress and roads and gather their strength. Any defensive efforts will prove futile, however, as the unfolding imagery shows.

Verse 2 seems out of place in the succession of images of the siege of a city, leading some to suggest it is a later gloss by an editor. However, it does provide some context for the destruction that is coming to Assyria – they are the 'ravagers' who have ravaged Jacob and Israel. Now Jacob and Israel will be restored while Assyria itself will be ravaged.

The invading army is a well-organised fighting machine, as depicted by their being dressed uniformly in red and costly scarlet, and driving shiny chariots that cause chaos in the streets (vv. 3–4). The king of Assyria attempts to assemble his troops to defend the city (v. 5) but his efforts are futile (v. 6). It's not entirely clear what is meant by the 'river gates' in verse 6. The city of Nineveh, on the east bank of the River Tigris, was defended by a wall and a system of moats and canals. A mountain stream ran through the city, providing water, and it is possible the wall was breached where this stream entered the city. The image of the palace collapsing signifies the collapse and invasion of the city, perhaps in part enabled by water destroying part of the wall.

Slave-women being led away may be a reference to temple prostitutes, beating their breasts at the removal of the goddess Ishtar from Nineveh (v. 7). The pool of water draining away (v. 8) artfully depicts the people of Nineveh fleeing and may also reference a possible flood of the city, given the image of the 'river gates' being breached (compare v. 6). Once the city is defeated, the invaders can loot its substantial treasures (v. 9).

The summary statement in verse 10 is a powerful succession of alliterative words, perhaps best captured in translation by the NRSV's 'devastation, desolation, and destruction!' The formerly formidable foe is rendered faint and fearful by the invading army. Nahum's vision of Nineveh's destruction was borne out in history, with its invasion and destruction carried out by an alliance of Babylonians, Medes and Scythians in 612BC.

4 The lion of Nineveh

With an ironic rhetorical question (v. 11), Nahum likens the king of Assyria to a lion, an appropriate image for a number of reasons. Lion hunting may have been a religious ritual activity of the king, and the palace at Nineveh featured decorative reliefs of royal lion hunts, panels of which may be seen at the British Museum today.

Rather than a lion hunter, however, the king of Assyria is now portrayed as a lion storing up 'prey' for his mate and children in his 'den' (v. 12) – the city of Nineveh. The image of the king of Assyria as a lion is also appropriate given the ferocity and cruelty of the Assyrians' treatment of the peoples they conquered. The 'prey' and 'torn flesh' in the image probably refer to the loot taken from these conquered peoples, wealth amassed over successful military campaigns and brought back to the city. But now, in a full and total reversal, the hunter becomes the lion and the lion becomes the prey.

It is also worth noting that in Amos, God's voice is paralleled with the lion's roar (Amos 3:8). Here in Nahum, the lion of Judah is about to vanquish the lion of Nineveh.

In a powerful first-person statement, the Lord of hosts, in his military capacity as commander of armies, declares himself to be 'against' Nineveh (v. 13). Chariot imagery, as well as the language of being 'cut off', is carried over from the first part of the chapter, forming a strong connection with what has gone before as well as continuing with the lion imagery here. The first-person announcement combined with all this imagery makes it absolutely clear that it is *Yahweh* who is going to act against Nineveh to burn up her chariots, devour her young lions with the sword and cut off her prey. It may be the Babylonian army and her allies that will carry out the destruction of the city, as was so graphically portrayed in 2:1–10, but it is the Lord of hosts who commands that army.

It is a fearsome thing to be considered an enemy of the Lord of hosts, and Nineveh has made herself such an enemy by her enduring evil and unimaginable cruelty.

5 Woe to the city of blood

These verses contain a woe oracle against Nineveh, beginning with three charges against her that will not go unpunished – bloodshed, deceit and plunder (v. 1). The sounds and sights of war are rapped out in a series of short, sharp phrases. Shocking images pile up like dead bodies, flashing past like the flash of sword and spear in the reader's imagination (vv. 2–3). The Assyrians' cruelty was infamous in the ancient world. They were known to pile up decapitated heads and bodies, such that the imagery of corpses piling up reflects their own cruelty to their enemies (v. 3).

Nineveh is then likened to two troublesome female figures in the ancient world – a prostitute and a witch – as an explanation for the charges against her (v. 4). She is pictured alluring other nations into false alliances that lead to their demise, as a prostitute allures a man to his downfall by her many charms (compare Proverbs 7). There may be some reference here to the city goddess Ishtar – idolatry is routinely likened to harlotry by the prophets.

The metaphor of a fallen city as a fallen woman is also used to great effect in both Hosea and Lamentations. Nineveh's punishment for her 'countless debaucheries' (v. 4) will be in kind, with her skirts lifted over her face so all can see her nakedness and shame (v. 5).

Although effective and evocative, this imagery of the city as a woman naked from the waist down being pelted with 'filth' (v. 6) is troubling, especially when it is emphasised once again that this treatment is unequivocally enacted by Yahweh (v. 5). As in 2:13, the Lord of hosts declares in the first person that he is 'against' her, and continues in the first person to describe what he will do to her (vv. 5–6). Indeed, the imagery is *meant* to shock and appal all who look upon the violated city (vv. 6–7), but perhaps it does so for different reasons to our 21st-century minds than for those who first witnessed the prophetic image.

The questions of verse 7 are rhetorical – none who have encountered Nineveh's great cruelty are likely to lament her demise. In a play on the prophet Nahum's name ('comfort'), no 'comforters' will be found for her (compare Lamentations 1:2, 16–17, 21).

6 A mortal wound

The question 'Are you better than Thebes?' (v. 8) draws together various ideas. Thebes, situated on the River Nile, with watery defences and multiple allies, fell to Assyria in 663BC. So in one sense, Nineveh *could* claim to be better and more powerful. But Nahum's point is that Nineveh is no better than the city she had defeated and treated so brutally – slaughtering infants, selling her nobles into slavery and chaining up her dignitaries (v. 10). Like Thebes, Nineveh used water for defence. Like Thebes, Nineveh was a powerful city associated with a supposedly powerful deity. Like Thebes, Nineveh reckoned on alliances with powerful allies. But the Assyrians were still able to conquer her, and so too will Nineveh be conquered, and treated in the same way she treated Thebes (v. 11). Like Thebes, Nineveh will flee from her enemies but be unable to resist them. Like ripe figs falling straight into the mouth of one who would consume them, so Nineveh's strongholds will fall to her enemy (v. 12). Nineveh's troops are then compared to women, which in the original context suggests weakness and vulnerability. In a possible reference to rape, her city gates are left wide open to enemy penetration (v. 13).

The Ninevites are called to prepare for a siege (compare 2:1 – drawing water, making bricks to shore up the defences. This is, however, an ironic call to arms, as no amount of preparation will make any difference when Yahweh has determined to destroy. Right there in the city the people will be destroyed, consumed by fire and cut off by the sword (v. 15).

The image of the locust is introduced in verse 15 and used in a variety of ways. Like locusts, the sword will devour or consume the people (v. 15). The people are encouraged to multiply like locusts, in another futile attempt at defending the city. The merchant traders of the city were numerous, but the moment there is trouble they shed their skin like the locust and flee (v. 16). And finally, the 'guards' and 'scribes' are like locusts that, while they may settle overnight, flee as soon as the scorching sun appears (v. 17).

The final words of judgement are reserved for the king of Assyria himself. He has failed in his duty to protect his people and he himself has suffered a mortal wound. No one will grieve him; rather, the nations clap their hands at his demise (v. 19).

Guidelines

Assyria's destruction is Judah's salvation. And what a destruction it is! There is none of Jonah's offer of repentance and salvation for Nineveh, only certain punishment. The Lord, who is jealous for Judah, will surely end their enemies. This is Nahum's message of comfort to Judah.

What 'comfort' might such a message bring to contemporary Christian readers? It may well be satisfying to think of situations where this dynamic could be translated today, but whether it is *Christian* to think of our enemies in the terms in which Nineveh is described is another question. Furthermore, the image of a vengeful and jealous God is neither comfortable nor comforting for many Christians.

One approach to such a confronting portrayal of God is perhaps to try more fully to appreciate the context into which Nahum speaks – a context of oppression and atrocities experienced under the Assyrians for 100 years. While the realities of war and foreign occupation may be a distant memory or a story in history books to many in the West, we may have some sympathy for Nahum's grim pleasure at Nineveh's impending doom if we attempt to put ourselves in those Judeans' shoes.

For those who have no power of their own, the vivid imagery of a God who has finally had enough, become angry and gone into battle for his people must be enormously comforting. When we consider the infamous cruelty of the Assyrian regime, we may concede that 'there is a legitimate celebration to be held over the destruction of evil on this earth' (Elizabeth Achtemeier, *Nahum–Malachi*, p. 28). But we must be cautious not to fall into the trap of an un-self-critical nationalism, recognising that we too harbour desires in our own hearts that would set us up in enmity towards God.

FURTHER READING

Elizabeth Achtemeier, *Nahum–Malachi* (Westminster John Knox, 1986).
Daniel Berrigan, *Minor Prophets, Major Themes* (Wipf and Stock, 2009).
Francisco O. García-Treto, 'The book of Nahum: Introduction, commentary, and reflections' in *The New Interpreter's Bible Commentary*, vol. V (2015), pp. 733–55.

Lamentations

Kate Bruce

Traditionally, this collection of five poems has been attributed to Jeremiah, due to similarities in phraseology and theme. This designated authorship is not conclusive; such overlap is likely with works originating in the same period of history. Most scholars agree that Lamentations is written by one person, or a group of people, who experienced the Babylonian invasion that smashed Jerusalem apart in 586BC, leaving Judah's people facing forced deportation, subjugation, persecution, starvation and death.

The provenance of the text is less important than the fact that it articulates profound experiences of suffering with courage, faith and honesty. It is used in the Jewish calendar to commemorate the two destructions of the temple, as well as being read in Holy Week liturgies, giving voice to the experience of desolation. Lamentations is no less relevant today than in 586BC.

Lamentations has features in common with the city-lament genre familiar in ancient Mesopotamia, such as poetic techniques, theme and mood, a female weeping figure and the attribution of destruction to the divine. However, the writer modifies aspects of the city-lament. Destruction is not wreaked by an unpredictable deity, but is a consequence of human sin. The divine warrior, Enlil, is replaced by Yahweh, and the weeping goddess becomes a female personification of Jerusalem. The note of restoration at the end of the city-lament is absent from Lamentations. Much of the latent hope in Lamentations is borne by the structural shape of the poems, which gives voice and containment to the raging darkness within.

These notes consider: the articulation of faith amid grief; the cost and consequence of sin; and the importance of listening in times of darkness. Threads of hope are identified in this tapestry of pain, and the reader is encouraged to bear with the exhaustion of another's suffering. Finally, the importance of lament as communal catharsis is considered. Alongside the readings from Lamentations, supplementary readings are given which bring in other angles, without muting the harsh cries of Lamentations.

Quotations are from the New Revised Standard Version.

1 Faith in the depths of grief

Lamentations 1

Chapters 1 and 2 both employ the same acrostic structure: 22 stanzas of three couplets, each beginning with successive letters of the Hebrew alphabet. Given there are 22 letters in this alphabet, the poem suggests structurally something of the all-encompassing dimensions of grief.

The narrator, like a modern newscaster, reads their piece (vv. 1–12). The opening word 'How' expresses horrified incredulity. Reading these verses, stark images from contemporary news media spring to mind: a child sits stunned, still and staring, grey with dust; streams of people depart the city under armed escort, clutching meagre possessions; close-up of an abandoned shoe.

We are offered flashbacks: temple festivals, colour, riches, royal pageantry. These images dissolve. We see a woman bowed and broken. Her persecutors mock her, throwing defiling taunts and sharp-edged stones. Her skirts are ripped and bloody, suggesting a more intimate brutalising.

Then she speaks direct to camera (vv. 12–22): 'Is it nothing to you, all you who pass by? Look and see if there is any sorrow like my sorrow' (v. 12). Physically, she trips, weighed down, stomach churning, tears streaming. Spiritually, she experiences God as angry, rejecting and casting her neighbours against her. Yesterday's lovers have betrayed her. The priests have starved to death. There is no one. Guilt and recrimination are her companions.

The hope lies in her articulation of grief, 'See, O Lord…' (v. 20). God is her audience. The lack of such a turning to God is clear in Jesus' lament over Jerusalem in Luke 13:34–35. We read of Jesus' deep compassion for Jerusalem and her children, as he longs to gather her chicks under his wings. But, he laments, 'You were not willing.' In contrast, the grieving, desolate woman of Lamentations 1 longs for comfort, acknowledges her responsibility in the depth of this calamity and hurls herself on the mercy of God. This is an act of deep and courageous faith, wrought in the depths of grief.

2 The cost and consequence of sin

This is a theologically troubling text. The image of God presented is in tension with the divine grace and love expressed in microcosm in the New Testament, such as in John 3:16. In this chapter, we encounter more of God's anger and the all-encompassing suffering Jerusalem experiences because of this. God 'has become like an enemy' (v. 5). He throws Israel down (v. 1); destroys mercilessly (v. 2); breaks strongholds (v. 2); cuts down (v. 3); consumes (v. 3); spurns and scorns (vv. 6–7); and 'has demolished without pity' (v. 17). The consequences of her sin speak against approaches to God which underplay divine holiness, shrinking God to manageable proportions.

There is no aspect of Jerusalem's life that has not been affected by the divine punishment. Politically and economically, Jerusalem is ruined. Domestic life is disordered: homes are destroyed, the dead lie in the street, children starve and we are presented with the macabre vision of cannibalism. We are spared nothing.

A primary cause of this destruction is the failure of religious leadership to speak truth: 'Your prophets… have not exposed your iniquity to restore your fortunes' (v. 14). In handling the images of Lamentations 2, we are reminded of the danger of treating sin as little more than a cheeky nibble on a cream cake. Sin's consequences are devastating; sin is an assault on the holiness of God, a gobbet of spit in the face of the divine.

The good news is that we have another lens through which to see how God deals with the reality of human sin, absorbing the consequences through the loving action of the incarnation and crucifixion of Jesus. We cannot rush too quickly from the wrenching agony of Lamentations to the resurrection, but neither can we act as though resurrection is not reality or as though God has not addressed sin's power. There is hope waiting in the wings. Paradoxically, the voice of lament is both a cry of anger at God and an expression of trust in God. Pastoral wisdom requires that this voice is allowed, for a time, space centre stage.

3 Listening in the darkness

Lamentations 3:1–18

The acrostic structure is intensified here. Each of the three lines of this chapter's stanzas begins with the same letter of the Hebrew alphabet. This has the effect of creating more tension, as the poet's anguished outcries butt into the constraints of the poetic form.

The opening verse presents us with a new voice – unambiguously male in the Hebrew. This offers a contrast to the female voice of the city. The suffering experienced cuts across gender. In the Hebrew, God is not referenced until verse 18, but the reader is in no doubt about the identity of the man's assailant. There are echoes here of Job 19:6–12, where God is portrayed as Job's adversary. Whereas Psalm 23 offers the image of the comforting rod, here the rod is an instrument of punishment, wielded in darkness. The poetic lines run over and the images press upon each other, presenting a superfluity of terror, baffling in its extremes.

The 'I' of this poem does not offer a theological rationale for his experience; he simply articulates his agonies. We are called to listen to him in his darkness. The immediacy of his anguish is not the right context for a theological treatise on the nature of suffering. Rather, it demands enduring compassion to listen without interruption, remembering that Job's friends were most helpful to him when they sat with him in silence (Job 2:13). Hope can be found in the darkest of places; its simplest expression comes in the form of open ears and a supportive hand. The latent hope in these verses lies in the reader taking seriously the man's anguished cries.

In June 2017, in the wake of the Grenfell Tower disaster in West London, the fury of some who experienced the devastation was palpable in the media. Of course, practical action needed to happen: a fair enquiry, and the provision of housing and support. However, none of this could replace the need to simply be present and listen without interruption as people gave voice to the hideous reality of their experiences.

In the 'text' of a situation of despair, we must ask ourselves how we can be hope-bearers: people who are willing to enter the darkness and listen.

4 Threads of hope in a tapestry of pain

Lamentations 3:21–57

The reader who hopes that Lamentations will resolve in a happy ending is going to be disappointed. However, if we read the poems as artworks expressing contrasting themes, rather than as a narrative heading to resolution, we will be able to trace threads of hope in this tapestry of pain.

Careful balance is needed here. Seizing upon the hope expressed must be done in such a way that the horror is not muted or negated. The mother bowed at her son's graveside, clutching a clod of earth, may find solace in resurrection hope, but this cannot negate the reality of her loss. This would amount to a denial of her wound in the rush for a pastoral salve. Hope is wrought in deep and difficult places and is never a quick fix.

However, a defiant voice of hope emerges in the midst of Lamentations, reminiscent of the wonderful and mysterious top note of faith bursting forth from the horrors of Job (Job 19:25–27), sung out in Handel's *Messiah*: 'I know that my Redeemer liveth.' Similarly, Lamentations 3 offers us this confident assertion: 'The steadfast love of the Lord never ceases, his mercies never come to an end' (v. 22). This is a remarkable expression of faith coming from the pit experience. It is as if the poet says, 'My reality is pain and grief and despair, but I know of another reality.' This is the deeper magic of Narnia. This is the perception of underground rivers in a scorched and barren landscape. These rivers can be named as Love, Divine Mercy, Hope, Patience, Penitence, Compassion, Trust and Faith. For a moment in Lamentations 3, these streams bubble up before flowing back into the earth, unseen but not unknown.

Even when we cannot see how restoration will come, we can identify the presence of God in human faith, courage, compassion and action. Unlike the writer(s) of Lamentations, we can be confident that ultimately hope bursts forth in the darkest of places, as it did for Mary in the garden, in the early morning light (John 20:11–16). Such resurrection hope gathers up the horrors of night, without denying them, and holds them against the hope that dawn will break and once again Jesus' presence will be known.

5 Bearing with the exhaustion of suffering

Lamentations 4:1–16

This fourth poem still conforms to an acrostic pattern, but the stanzas are shorter and only the first line of each follows the pattern, lessening the emotional intensity. There is something dirge-like in the mood. This poem makes less use of enjambment, a poetic device that allows ideas to overrun their lines, creating a sense of urgency. This poem lacks that energy. There is a feeling that the poet is emotionally stunned. The sense of exhaustion is palpable. Each line is a snapshot in a photo album of pain; there is a sense of the poet pointing to this, and this, and this, in a matter-of-fact litany.

This is reminiscent of some Holocaust literature, for example Elie Wiesel's book *Night*, which recounts unimaginable horror in a matter-of-fact tone. Wiesel describes, on arrival at a death camp, seeing the bodies of babies being tipped from a truck into a burning trench. Similarly, the writer of this poem describes in simple language how the thirsty infant's tongue sticks to the roof of its mouth, children beg in vain for food (v. 4) and 'the hands of compassionate women have boiled their own children; they became their food' (v. 10). The tension between the subject matter and the dirge-like recitation is hard to bear.

The experience of reading these verses is not dissimilar to that of staying with a person deep in the grip of depression. There is heaviness here: the weight of bearing with relentless, crushing suffering. Hope seems to have run underground. However, latent hope can still be located in the dogged desire of the poet to tell their story and in the willingness of the reader/listener to stay present.

Bearing with the exhaustion of another's suffering requires hope in a promise of something beyond the immediate experience. It is an expression of trust in God, even in the midst of great difficulty. It is a form of prayerful defiance of darkness. Weeping with those who weep is the highest expression of compassion. When Jesus saw Mary and the others weeping at the tomb of Lazarus, he wept with them (John 11:32–35).

6 Lament as communal catharsis

The final poem is marked by the disappearance of the earlier acrostic patterns, signalling a slowing down. The reader familiar with the city-lament expects celebration at the return of the gods. Those of us familiar with the happily-ever-after endings of comedy and romance may well expect a note of resolution. However, what we are given is a prayer of communal lament, laden with longing and demand. This poem, like Psalm 80 – another communal lament – offers the catharsis of a community together in grief.

Together, the people recount their suffering. They have lost everything (v. 2); they are vulnerable and enslaved (vv. 3–5). They have made pacts with Egypt and Assyria and they bear the cost of such unfaithfulness (v. 6). Women are sexually violated, princes and elders humiliated, and young boys oppressed (vv. 11–14). In short, 'The joy of our hearts has ceased; our dancing has turned to mourning' (v. 15).

The final four verses articulate the question at the heart of all experiences of profound suffering alongside deep faith: 'Why have you forgotten us… [and] forsaken us?' (v. 20). God, where are you?

Ending the poem with a question addressed to God creates a sense of expectancy. The question of whether God has utterly rejected and abandoned his people with anger beyond measure (v. 22) is itself a demand that God responds in accordance with his merciful character. Implicitly, the poem invites God's response of steadfast love. This is an act of great courage, since the invitation comes from the lived experience of an unresolved story.

A cursory glance at most contemporary hymn books will reveal a liturgical imbalance. Songs of triumph and praise abound, while hymns of lament are relatively few. As we have seen, individual and communal lament is faithful and cathartic. The open-ended messiness of lament reflects something of the experience of faith wrought in the crucible of suffering. As such, Lamentations is a vital resource today, an expression of defiant faith and catharsis.

Guidelines

Does the book of Lamentations have a place in our shared liturgical life, or is it just too raw to appear at the 11.00 am service? How might it be used?

The consequences of sin are clearly expressed in Lamentations. Has sin become an old-fashioned concept in the life of the church? These notes describe sin as 'a gobbet of spit in the face of the divine'. Devise your own images for sin. What are the theological consequences of minimising sin?

The poems are written by a writer or writers who understood the possibilities and richness of poetic language. What is the place of poetry in the life of faith? What are its benefits compared to prose?

What might the preacher have to learn from poetic expression?

To what extent does the poem's refusal to offer an easy response to the experience of suffering inform our response to those in deep darkness?

Lamentations 4 invites us to listen to the experience of profound exhaustion in the depth of suffering. Bring to mind someone you know personally or have heard about in the news who faces profound pain, and pray for them. Try to enter into their experience from their perspective. If you can, reduce the distance between your experience and theirs by articulating your prayer, on their behalf, in the first person.

Write a prayer of lament concerning a situation you are experiencing or one known to you. Remember that the lament prayer gives powerful voice to the reality of suffering before turning to an expression of hope in God, based on past experience, crying out to God and trusting God on that basis.

Consider the 'text' of a situation of despair and ask yourself how you can be a hope-bearer.

Take time to review the index of your church hymn book/musical resources. Are laments being used in the sung life of the church? What is gained/lost by the use of communal lament?

The birth of special children

David Spriggs

Jesus' birth is presented to us as unique. From conception to delivery, this birth is marked out as highly unusual, noteworthy and significant. Of course, every birth is special and unique, especially for the parents and family. But Jesus' birth is presented in scripture as completely remarkable.

In different ways and in different times, other children's births are also made to stand out in scripture. In this week's notes, we shall consider some of these, and this will help us appreciate the richness of Christ's birth in a special way. Many of Israel's most significant leaders are noteworthy in this way (but not all of them – think of Saul and David). Hence we will consider Isaac, Joseph, Moses, Samuel and John the Baptist. Unfortunately, we will not have time to reflect on Samson (but please read Judges 13:2–25), or the mysterious children in Isaiah 7:14–16 and 8:1–4, 16–18, or the hint about Jeremiah (see Jeremiah 1:5). It is worth noting that, apart from that of Samuel, the births of the prophets are not considered at all.

What is also important to note in passing, however, is that by no means all Israel's leaders are given special significance through some kind of birth account. There is none for Noah or Abraham, Joshua or Gideon, David or Saul; none for Elijah or Elisha. Hence it is clear that a 'special' birth or conception is no requirement for being a highly important person in God's strategy. Indeed, perhaps on the contrary, a divine call is more significant than a remarkable birth. Yet the fact remains that Jesus' conception and birth are exceptional. If we are to garner some of the implications of this, we need to familiarise ourselves with how Jesus' birth resembles and resonates with other remarkable births.

Unless otherwise stated, quotations are from the New Revised Standard Version.

1 Isaac

Genesis 18:1–15; 21:1–7

'The Lord appeared to Abraham…' Of course, this is not the first time that God has appeared to Abraham, but this one is full of mystery. We are not given a clue as to how God 'appeared' in terms of what he looked like, but we are given the process: the story goes on to recount how Abraham looks up and there are suddenly three men there. He persuades them to stay with him. Sarah becomes involved in preparing a meal for them. Soon their voices become the voice of the Lord, and he promises Abraham that within a year his wife will have a son.

If the first passage is full of mystery, then the second is full of mysteriously prosaic statements about that mystery: 'Sarah conceived and bore Abraham a son in his old age, at the time of which God had spoken to him' (21:2).

The first seven words could have been said about any birth of a son, but the second half of the sentence takes us into the heart of the mystery.

'In his old age', further expanded as 'Abraham was a hundred years old when his son Isaac was born to him' (21:5), underlines the strangeness of this birth. It is unnatural for a son to be born to such an aged father, and the earlier passage emphasises this strangeness from Sarah's perspective – she is post-menopausal and cannot conceive any longer. As a woman, she is so aware of this reality that it prompts her to laugh. The claim that she will become pregnant is ridiculous! Was it then a strange conception?

But this does not take us to the heart of the mystery, which is to do with the origins and purpose of this birth. The birth is written into the plan of God – for Abraham, yes, but also for the world. The comprehensive promises of God for the blessing of the world (Genesis 12:1–3) depend on this strange birth. In this respect, it is a close parallel to the birth of Jesus. There is no angelic choir announcing Isaac's birth to the world, no heavenly claim that this is the way God will save the world (contrast Luke 2:8–20), although there is a hint or two: the birth took place at the time God had promised and Isaac was circumcised as God had commanded. Most importantly of all, without Isaac there could be no future as promised by God.

2 Joseph

Does Joseph deserve a place in this gallery of special births? His birth is not even mentioned directly in this passage, where for the first time the focus is on him. He is introduced to us as already 17 years old! But we do glean something about his conception, not that we are told anything directly. Here is the key verse: 'Now Israel loved Joseph more than any of his other children, because he was the son of his old age' (v. 3).

Yet the story tells us there must be more to it than this. Jacob had another son after Joseph, for Benjamin was also born to Rachel. Therefore Joseph was not the last of his children born in his old age. This is not a sufficient explanation, even if it is a partial one! Rachel was Jacob's favourite wife, indeed his first love. He had worked 14 years to obtain her, but the time flew by. She was 'graceful and beautiful' (29:15–19). But there is still more. Rachel had not conceived, whereas her sister Leah, who was also married to Jacob through her father's deceit, had, and this caused a breach in Jacob and Rachel's love relationship (30:1–2). Various intrigues were utilised to try to patch up this brokenness until 'God heeded her and opened her womb. She conceived and bore a son and said, "God has taken away my reproach"' (37:22–23).

Although it is not spelled out, Joseph was Jacob's favourite son because he had put right the painful breach between Jacob and Rachel. Joseph's birth brought to an end the struggle, and perhaps also the guilt Jacob felt because he could not satisfy the longing of his wife's broken heart (see 30:2).

3 Moses

Verse 2 says, 'The woman conceived and bore a son; and when she saw that he was a fine baby, she hid him for three months.'

When we read these words on their own, they seem rather strange. Why did she hide this new baby for three months, especially as 'he was a fine baby'? If he had been deformed, then maybe he would have been killed at birth. If he had been a girl, then the mother might have hidden her baby to keep her alive, for in some cultures girls are not wanted and are killed. In another culture, she might have hidden him because she was an unmarried mother and having a baby would have brought shame on her and her family, or even on her husband-to-be (see Matthew 1:19). At the very least, she might have been forced to hand the child over for adoption. In another culture, it might have been because she had fallen in love with and married someone from a different caste or tribe. But none of this applies; she was married and married within her tribe (v. 1).

All was perfectly in order. So this mother was not ashamed, nor were her tribe. But her son *was* in danger. He was to play a pivotal role in the deliverance of God's people, the founding of the Hebrew nation and so, in the fulfilment of God's promises to Abraham, the blessing of the whole world. But he lived under an oppressive regime. The king of Egypt had ordered that all male children born to the Hebrews must be killed (1:15–16).

The Hebrew midwives, however, 'feared God' rather than the Pharaoh (1:17). The mother of Moses also feared God more than the Pharaoh and protected her son. The strangeness about this story lies not in the conception, nor in the birth itself, but in the preservation of this very vulnerable child.

Two other women are involved in this preservation. First, the baby's sister, who watches as, placed in a water-proofed basket, Moses floats down the Nile, and then, perhaps most oddly but also appropriately, one of Pharaoh's own daughters (vv. 3–10).

The strangeness in this birth story lies in the fact that four women are involved in preserving the life of Israel's greatest leader. Without female courage, compassion and ingenuity, there would have been no Moses. Without the response of a royal figure to the cry of a child (v. 6), he might well have died. How wonderfully God works through natural feelings and responses to ensure his plan of salvation comes to fruition!

4 Samuel

1 Samuel 1:1–20

This account begins in a very bland way, with the introduction of a 'certain man' (v. 1). We get the usual geographical and genealogical details and eventually his name – Elkanah. There is nothing remarkable about him; he's not a Levite or a member of the Aaronic priesthood. In fact, the only reason we know about him, in contrast to his thousands of peers, is that he had a wife called Hannah. We have to wait to be introduced to her, and then she is revealed to us as a woman in a difficult situation. Elkanah has two wives and one of them has children; Hannah does not.

We do learn Elkanah is a devout man – for he goes to the temple at Shiloh to worship annually. He is also unusual in that, although Hannah has failed to produce any children, let alone a male heir, he treats her with special favour, 'because he loved her' (v. 5). All this did was make Hannah's life more miserable; his other wife, Peninnah, used to mock Hannah because of her infertility.

Then, in her desperation and need, she turns to God in prayer. Participation in the sacrifice, even her double portion, has failed to satisfy her need: 'In deep anguish Hannah prayed to the Lord, weeping bitterly' (v. 10, NIV).

She makes a vow; she keeps on praying, praying in her heart not just with words. Indeed, so great is her distress that, although her lips are forming the words, no sound emerges. How is her deep piety and desperate longing perceived? The attentive priest Eli accuses her of being drunk! To his lasting credit, he eventually listens to her explanation and accepts it, affirming it before God.

So 'in due time Hannah conceived and bore a son' (v. 20). Was this a miraculous conception or birth? These words, being so prosaic, suggest not. Unlike Mary's pregnancy, which came unsought and inconveniently early, Hannah's comes unduly late and is the result of her soul's travail and deep prayer. But what she does share in common with Mary is the cost to her of this birth: her son will never truly be hers; he is dedicated to God – God's very special gift, but not hers to possess. She makes the ultimate sacrifice and hands him into the care of Eli for dedicated service to God.

5 John the Baptist

Luke 1:5–25

Several of our special births provide a prelude to that of John the Baptist. For, like Sarah, Rachel and Hannah, Elizabeth could not conceive. With typical Lukan sensitivity, this is presented to us as a shared burden with her husband. 'But *they* had no children…' (v. 7a, my emphasis). Unlike those earlier wives, Elizabeth was spared the pain of seeing another woman bear her husband children, or even being rebuked and abused by other wives for her failure. But the hopelessness of the situation is underlined through the words 'and both were getting on in years' (v. 7b).

Eventually, we are given a glimpse into the real cost of her childlessness: 'This is what the Lord has done for me when he looked favourably on me and took away the disgrace I have endured among my people' (v. 24).

'Disgrace' indicates that Elizabeth had carried her childlessness as a stigma: she was not like other wives; every time she had seen them give birth, she felt her failure. 'Disgrace' indicates being out of favour with God, with all the uncertainty that brought. Why, as the wife of a priest and indeed a descendant of Aaron in her own right, was she not blessed by God? What had she done wrong? She would carry the additional burden that this also brought shame on her husband Zechariah and meant that there would be no son to follow him in his priestly office.

Yet, in spite of this predicament, 'both of them were righteous before God' (v. 6). Maybe we are provided with this information to alleviate any sense that the barrenness was the consequence of a disobedient life or some kind of divine chastisement. Indeed, the position of this statement before we are told of Elizabeth's childlessness strongly suggests that.

Yet, in many ways, the contrasts with Sarah, Rachel and Hannah are remarkable. Unlike with Hannah, we are not told that Elizabeth pleaded with God to remove the disgrace, although the angel's confirmation that 'Your prayer has been heard' (v. 13) to Zechariah indicates that at least he had shared his sorrow and made this a request to God. Unlike with Sarah and Rachel, there was no recourse with Elizabeth to alleviate the disgrace through the use of surrogate wives. As with Abraham (and Sarah), there is an angelic visitation to make the announcement, but this is restricted entirely to Zechariah – there is no way Elizabeth can listen in.

All we get is a single statement, following the return of Zechariah to his own home after his priestly service in Jerusalem was completed: 'After those days his wife Elizabeth conceived' (v. 24).

For five months – until she was sure the conception would deliver – 'she remained in seclusion'. No triumphal announcements, even though, as with Sarah, God promised an amazing future for her son (vv. 14–17).

6 Jesus

As we reflect finally on the way the birth of Jesus is presented, I invite you to consider this unique birth in the light of these other significant births in the Bible.

Unlike with Rachel, Hannah and Zechariah, there is no indication that Mary and Joseph had been pleading with God (in Abraham and Sarah's case, this is less clear but likely) – rather the contrary. As with Abraham and Zechariah, there is an angelic messenger involved, but, even though the message is even more unbelievable, there is no hint of disbelief on the part of Mary or Joseph (although Joseph has his own struggles about it all).

On the positive side, with these other miraculous birth stories, while there are many indications that there was some divine initiative, none of them implies there was no role for the human father, nor is the conception attributed to the direct intervention of God, which 'she was found to be with child by the Holy Spirit' (v. 18) indicates very strongly.

In several of the Old Testament illustrations, the conception and birth put right a difficult situation for the mother (abuse from another wife or shame within the community); here, the opposite is the case. The realisation that Mary was pregnant was the source of embarrassment and shame rather than release from it.

In several of the previous births, the unlikeliness of a child is associated with old age and the observation that the parents were past childbearing; here, it is again the opposite: Mary is clearly very young and there has been no attempt to conceive. This is presented to us as a divine initiatory choice.

Naming the child is a theme in the case of Moses (Exodus 2:10), Samuel (1 Samuel 1:20) and John the Baptist (Luke 1:13, 59–63), and also occurs with the prophets (e.g. Isaiah and his children, or Hosea and his), and in many other situations. But there is no consistency. With Moses, his naming is attributed to the Egyptian princess; with Hannah, it is her initiative; and with both, there is an explanation of the name; only with John the Baptist is there a divine command – but without any explanation. In the case of Jesus, it is both a divine command and given an explanation.

What we discover by contextualising the account of the birth of Jesus within the unusual and significant births recounted in the Bible is that Jesus' conception and birth do not follow a well-worn pattern or trajectory.

Even in this respect, Jesus is presented in a unique way. We do well to observe the differences rather than assume similarities.

Guidelines

Many Bible authors were well aware that childlessness could be a huge burden for couples who longed for a child.

Pray for couples who are desperate for children, and for those around them who share these deep concerns, but give thanks for those who research and provide ways (such as IVF) to give hope.

The birth of Jesus also makes clear that there can be problems for unmarried mothers. While many couples today plan for children prior to marriage, there are still many women who find themselves with unplanned pregnancies. Pray for all who have to make difficult decisions about abortion, adoption, fostering and provision for the new baby within an extended family. Pray for fathers who (for very different reasons, perhaps), like Joseph, are shocked to discover their partner is pregnant.

As Christmas approaches, pray for all children whose lives are in danger or who are deprived of the full love and support that God intends for our families. Pray for all organisations, such as Children's Society and Spurgeons Children's Charity, who seek to support vulnerable children and families.

Advent in Luke: introducing Luke 1—2

Steve Walton

Luke's first two chapters are populated with a series of fascinating characters whose role is to shed light on the coming of Jesus. These chapters have a strong Old Testament feel, as we meet godly Jews: Zechariah and Elizabeth, Simeon and Anna. We encounter the temple as a key setting, for both Zechariah, and Simeon and Anna – and thus for Jesus, Mary and Joseph as they come for Mary's purification after childbirth. We hear songs which echo scripture on the lips of Mary and Zechariah, songs of rejoicing and praise that God is now acting to save his people. We learn of the coming of the last of the prophets, John, the son of Elizabeth and Zechariah.

The coming of Jesus is portrayed in these chapters through vivid images and striking phrases: he will bring light, he will save, he will redeem, he will bring glory; he is saviour, Lord, Messiah, Davidic king. Watch out for these images and phrases and keep track of how Luke uses them to build up a portrait of who Jesus is and what he has come to do.

Watch out, too, for these human characters who are Jesus' 'supporting cast'. They offer us models of what it means to live with God, and sometimes what it means to fail to trust God or to recognise what God is doing. We can see ourselves frequently in these people, for they are deeply realistic portraits of the ordinary human beings Jesus comes to save.

Quotations are from the New Revised Standard Version.

1 Zechariah's story: promise, unbelief and fulfilment

Luke 1:1–25

How does a godly man end up silenced by an angel because of his unbelief? That's Zechariah's story here, and it centres on his encounter with the angel in the temple.

Zechariah is not only a priest, but a devout man, married to a devout wife, Elizabeth (v. 6). The blot on the landscape is that they are childless (v. 7), since children were understood as a mark of God's blessing (e.g. Psalm 127:3–5). Thus not to have children was surprising for a godly couple – hence Elizabeth speaks of her 'disgrace' as a childless woman (v. 25). There are, of course, biblical examples of godly couples who were childless having children after God's intervention, such as Abraham and Sarah (Genesis 18:9–15; 21:1–7) or Jacob and Rachel (Genesis 30:1, 22–24). And as a priest, Zechariah would know these stories.

Yet when the angel appears to Zechariah and promises in the plainest terms that he and Elizabeth will have a son who will be a great man of God (vv. 11–17), Zechariah's response is to imply that this is impossible (v. 18). He points to his and his wife's age as counter-evidence to the promise. What was he thinking? Here is a priest whose reaction to God's word is to doubt, and to ask for more evidence than God's promise: 'How will I know that this is so?' The angel diagnoses his unbelief (v. 20).

Zechariah is not the first in scripture to doubt God's words – the first temptation in the Bible was when the serpent said to Eve, 'Did God say...?' (Genesis 3:1), and then flatly contradicted God's words: 'You will not die' (Genesis 3:4; compare 3:3). When God moves, he moves by his word of promise, and invites and calls people to trust him. Failure to trust leads to divine discipline, so Zechariah is silenced for the period of Elizabeth's pregnancy (v. 20), and faces the embarrassment of being unable to speak anything about his vision (vv. 21–22).

God's word of promise is fulfilled as Elizabeth becomes pregnant (v. 24), for God is not dependent on human trust for his purposes to be carried out. God is preparing the way for the coming of a greater child, Jesus, for whom Elizabeth and Zechariah's son John will prepare the way (vv. 16–17).

2 Mary's story: promise, trust and prophecy

Luke loves to pair a man and a woman and tell their stories in parallel; here Mary parallels Zechariah, whom we met yesterday. As so often with Luke, it's the woman who comes off better as the positive example!

Both Mary and Zechariah receive an angel's visit, and both are given the angel's promise of a child (vv. 28–33, 11–17). Both ask a 'How' question – but there is a difference. Mary's question is about how God's words can be brought to effect, since she is a virgin (v. 34), by contrast with Zechariah's question as to how *he* can know (v. 18). Mary asks about the means by which God's word will be carried out, but Zechariah asks about his own certainty concerning God's word. That's why the angel's response to Mary explains the means: the Holy Spirit will cause her to become pregnant (v. 35). The angel also encourages Mary that God can and will carry out his word, for Elizabeth's pregnancy shows the amazing things which God can do (vv. 36–37). Mary's full statement of trust follows – trust in God's word through the angel: 'Let it be with me according to your word' (v. 38). God's word calls for trust from his people – Mary models that trust, and Zechariah models lack of it.

God is working out an amazing plan through Mary's pregnancy – a plan to bring to fulfilment his promises to Mary's ancestor, David. Her son is going to be the promised ruler over the people of Israel ('the house of Jacob', v. 33). Here, we hear the echo of the prophet Nathan's promise to David that there would always be a descendant of David on Israel's throne (2 Samuel 7:12–16). Mary's son is to be that one, and even greater: he himself will reign *for ever* (v. 33).

Mary's response is not only to state her trust, but to offer her praise. Her 'Magnificat' (vv. 46–55) sings with the joy of what God is doing and will do through this child. Lowly Israel will be lifted up (v. 52). God's promises to Abraham will be fulfilled (v. 55) – and we, as Christian readers, can recognise that they include God's promise that, through Abraham's family, all the nations of the earth will be blessed (Genesis 12:1–3). God's arms will embrace the world through Mary's son, Jesus.

3   Elizabeth and Zechariah's story: promise fulfilled

Luke 1:57-80

Luke's focus switches back to his first couple, Elizabeth and Zechariah, at the point of their son's birth (v. 57). Elizabeth acts in obedience to the angel's word and wants the child to be called John (vv. 60, 13), against the tradition to use a relative's name (v. 61). Now Zechariah learns that obedience to God's word produces freedom: when he writes that the child is to be called John, he is able to speak again (vv. 63–64). How will he use that freedom? How will he fill the silence he has kept during the long months of pregnancy with words?

Zechariah's words are praise and prophecy. He speaks God's praise, for he rejoices that God has fulfilled his promise of a son (v. 64), and he speaks prophecy inspired by the Holy Spirit in his 'Benedictus' (vv. 67–79). Luke's penchant for pairing a man and a woman appears again: just as Mary has spoken a praise song (vv. 46–55), now Zechariah does the same. A number of themes overlap between the two songs, such as: God's covenant promises to Abraham (vv. 73, 55); God's move now to save his people (vv. 68–69, 47); God's mercy for his people (vv. 72, 50). Can you find others?

At the end of his song, Zechariah uses a striking image of what John's prophetic ministry will mean. John will prepare for the Lord's coming, as Luke will say further in quoting Isaiah 40:3–5 (Luke 3:4–6). John prepares for one Zechariah calls 'the Lord' – and that is Jesus. In Isaiah 40, the Lord who is coming is God himself, and the same is true with Jesus – in Jesus, the eternal God comes to the world following his forerunner and prophet John.

This coming is like 'the dawn from on high' breaking (v. 78). Sunrise in Israel/Palestine is quite something: one moment it's dark, and then suddenly it's light as dawn breaks and a glorious sun comes over the horizon and lights up the land. It brings back warmth to enable plants to grow and people to thrive – it's the very opposite of the darkness of night. That's what the coming of Jesus will be like, says Zechariah – new light and new life!

4 Mary and Joseph's story: promise fulfilled

Luke 2:1–20

Luke frequently teaches by contrast, as we saw in the contrast between Zechariah's and Mary's responses to the angels' messages. Here there are at least two such contrasts.

First, Luke locates the birth of Jesus in the context of world history, and thus compares Jesus with the emperor. Augustus is the emperor, and a census is called (vv. 1–2). There is some dispute over which census Luke means: the first recorded census in Judea was in AD6, when Quirinius was governor of Syria, but that is nine years after the probable birth of Jesus in 4BC. However, the word translated 'first' in most English Bibles can also mean 'before' – it is used in John 1:15, when John says Jesus 'was before me'. So we should translate here: 'This was the census which took place before Quirinius was governor of Syria.' Alas, as is frequently the case in ancient history, there are gaps in our knowledge: we don't have full records of all the censuses which took place, so we don't know the precise date of this census – but this translation does make historical sense of what Luke writes.

This location in world history contrasts Augustus and Jesus. Augustus became emperor and was celebrated as 'saviour' of the empire, which encompassed most of the then-known world; whereas Jesus was born in obscurity but was to bring salvation which would extend to the whole earth (vv. 11, 14).

Second, there is a contrast between Jesus' true status and his humble origins. His true status is revealed by the angel to the shepherds (v. 11): he is a Davidic descendant, a king for Israel; he is a saviour, who will deliver his people into true freedom; he is the Messiah, God's chosen instrument for restoring and renewing his people – and thus greater than John, who prepares the way for him; and, climactically, he is *the* Lord – in Jesus, God himself is coming to visit his people. Yet, by contrast, Jesus is born in an ordinary home – the word frequently translated 'inn' (v. 7) more probably means a guest room in an ordinary home. There was no such room available, and so they were in the middle of the single living room where the whole family lived and slept with their animals. The manger in which Jesus was laid was there to feed the animals – perhaps sheep, goats or cattle. Jesus' birth is in an ordinary place, as one of us – he comes as a human to save humanity.

5 Simeon and Anna's story: promise fulfilled

Luke 2:21–40

Modern Western societies tend to write older people off; they are retired and withdraw from public life and work. By contrast, older people were valued and greatly respected in the ancient world for their wisdom. Here, we meet two godly elderly people who have a living hope in God – and again we see Luke pairing a man and a woman to teach us, as well as to provide the two witnesses required to establish a case in court (Deuteronomy 19:15).

Simeon is a man soaked in the Holy Spirit – three times Luke draws attention to this (vv. 25, 26, 27). Thus his words concerning Jesus carry great weight as he speaks in the temple. Jesus is all that Simeon has waited for: Jesus means 'God saves', and Simeon sees him as God's salvation in person (v. 30). Not only that, but this salvation will extend to include even those who are not Jewish – Gentiles; they will have their lives lit up by the coming of Jesus, and see things as they truly are (v. 32a). It is worth comparing 1:78–79, where Zechariah speaks of the coming of Jesus as providing light for the people of Israel, for Simeon will also say that Jesus brings glory to Israel (v. 32b). What Jesus comes to do is comprehensive and inclusive – it is for 'all peoples' (v. 31). The stage on which Jesus will operate is growing, story by story, to include the whole world.

Anna is known as a prophet, and comes from one of the ten lost northern tribes, Asher (v. 36). This signals that Jesus comes to bring back together the broken twelve tribes of Israel, as Ezekiel had pictured with two sticks being joined together (Ezekiel 37:16–19). Like Simeon, she reacts to Jesus with praise to God (vv. 38, 28), and connects Jesus to the hope for God redeeming (setting free) the city of Jerusalem, the heart of Israel, then in the hands of the occupying Romans.

And yet this salvation is not without cost: the shadow of the cross hangs over even the infant Jesus. Simeon warns that Jesus will be opposed, and that Mary's heart will experience great pain (vv. 34–35). Our picture of the mission of Jesus is growing through these godly elderly people.

6 Jesus, Mary and Joseph's story: panic, puzzlement and putting God first

Luke 2:41–52

Luke skips over twelve years to this remarkable story. Here, Jesus' boyhood seems to be thoroughly normal, as a young villager who spends time with his neighbours and friends, to the extent that his parents did not miss him for a whole day as they travelled home from the Passover festival in Jerusalem (v. 44).

When they finally track him down, they have two surprises: first, that he is in the temple, and second, that he is engaging at a level well beyond his years with the teachers (vv. 46–47). And now we hit the nub of the issue: whose child is Jesus? Mary and Joseph consider him theirs: Luke calls them 'his parents', and Mary speaks of 'your father and I' (v. 48). As readers of Luke 1, we know that Joseph is Jesus' stepfather, rather than his biological father (1:35), and Jesus makes that clear in his response to his mother's agitated question. Most versions translate this as 'I must be in my Father's *house*' (v. 49), although there is no word for 'house' in the text. It is possible that we should translate it as '[engaged] in the *things* of my Father' or 'about my Father's *business*'; Jesus is then indicating that his focus is his relationship to God, his true Father, and carrying out the mission he has from God. However, Jesus is explaining why they did not need to search for him (v. 49) – they should have known where to look. So it may be that 'the things of my Father' at least includes a location, the temple as God's 'house'.

His parents still don't get it (v. 50), but Jesus is as obedient to the law as his parents. Just as they kept the law by circumcising Jesus and bringing an offering to the temple for Mary's purification (vv. 21–24), Jesus submits to them (v. 51) as the commandment says: 'Honour your father and mother' (Exodus 20:12). No wonder Luke observes that Jesus' growth and development are fully rounded: he grows intellectually, in age, and in relation to God and humans (v. 52).

Guidelines

The identity and mission of Jesus loom large in these chapters, as Luke sets the scene for Jesus' public ministry, which is detailed from 3:21 onwards. Luke uses a number of key images and terms to describe Jesus and what he has come to do, and they range widely. Read through the two chapters and note down these images and words, and reflect on what they tell you about who Jesus is and what he is doing today, as well as how he conducted his earthly ministry. How do these characteristics and activities of Jesus have an impact on you, your daily life, your family and your church? Make these a focus for prayer over the days ahead.

The characters around Jesus in these chapters invite reflection too, for they model what it means to face in God's direction or not. Frequently, as we have noticed, Luke does this by pairing people to show a comparison or contrast. Choose one pair and consider what positive and negative lessons they offer concerning what it means to walk with God, and then ask how far you, and others around you, are like them in both positive and negative ways. Talk with someone who knows you very well, such as a spouse or a close friend – often they have a realistic view of us which can help those of us who are over-negative or over-optimistic about ourselves. Give thanks to God for the work he is doing in your life in the positive features, and ask God to work more and more to transform you when you are not yet the person he calls you to be.

Reflecting on the stories in Luke 2:41–52 concerning Jesus' childhood, consider your roles as children and parents/godparents (if you have children/godchildren). How far are you ready to see your children or godchildren as 'on loan' from God, and to set them free to be the people God calls them to be? How far do you honour your parents, even when they don't get what God wants you to do and to be?

FURTHER READING

T. France, *Luke*, Teach the Text series (Baker, 2013).

Tom Wright, *Luke for Everyone* (SPCK, 2001).

Human flourishing in John's Gospel

Andrew Lincoln

There is much talk, both popular and academic, about human flourishing. We all aspire to a full and flourishing life. Indeed, that is what many mean when they talk about being spiritual, even if not religious. Sometimes circumstances conspire so that we can do no more than adopt survival mode, or our own poor choices may result in times of languishing, but the yearning to live more fully does not disappear.

What has this to do with the Gospel of John? Isn't its account of the life of Jesus, in the form of an ancient biography, meant to persuade readers to believe its claims about him, rather than to cater for what they consider to be their need for fulfilment? The suspicion behind this question is only partially justified. Indeed, this Gospel's statement of purpose reads, 'But these are written so that you may believe that Jesus is the Messiah, the Son of God,' yet then continues, 'and that through believing you may have life in his name' (20:31). It turns out that readers are being offered life, indeed life in abundance (10:10), but that trust in the particular identity of Jesus is key to experiencing it; enjoyment of it will not simply be on their own terms.

What, then, does this Gospel's vision of a full and flourishing life entail? This week's readings have been selected to enable exploration of just a few of its aspects that, on further reflection, may feed into the ongoing tradition of Christian thought about the good life and its encounter with rival contemporary views of what constitutes a life worth living.

Quotations are from the New Revised Standard Version.

1 Wine in abundance

John 2:1–11

The account of Jesus' first major deed or sign (v. 11) is designed to have a special impact on readers, to signal to them what this main character is all about, and to set the tone for the rest of the narrative. Turning water into wine at a wedding is not a miraculous response to a dire human need, though the lack of provision of sufficient wine would have constituted a serious loss of honour for the bridegroom. The sign has more to do with generous giving than with necessity, a point reinforced by the amount of wine the miracle produces. Jesus changed into wine the water in six stone jars, each containing from 20 to 30 gallons (v. 6). So the guests at this village wedding, who have already been drinking enough that the wine has run out, now have made available to them the equivalent of over 900 of the 75 centilitre bottles with which we are familiar. Wine was 'created to make people happy' (Sirach 31:27), 'to gladden the human heart' (Psalm 104:15), and its provision by Jesus in excessive abundance indicates that his mission is to enable people to celebrate life and its festivities with joy.

But in Jewish thought, wine in abundance was also used in depictions of the salvation of the end time – 'the mountains shall drip sweet wine, and all the hills shall flow with it' (Amos 9:13) – and of the Messianic age when 'on one vine will be a thousand branches, and one branch will produce a thousand clusters, and one cluster will produce a thousand grapes, and one grape will produce a cor of wine' (2 Baruch 29:5). Just one grape will produce about 48 British gallons of wine!

The story of water into wine, then, depicts Jesus as God's Messiah who is inaugurating in the present the economy of the end time, with its abundance and joy. While Jesus' offer clearly takes in the good things of life rather than denigrating them, how it differs from that of rival claimants to be the source of abundance, such as Dionysus, famed as the god of wine, or the Roman emperors, depicted as emulating Dionysus in their roles as providers of life in abundance, remains to be seen from the rest of the story.

2 Bread of life

In another sign that indicates his mission is about sustaining life, Jesus has supplied miraculously another staple of the Mediterranean diet in feeding 5,000 people: bread (6:1–15). While the water into wine account received no additional explicit interpretation, the feeding is followed by a discourse that draws out its significance. Because this account evokes the story of Israel receiving manna in the wilderness (compare vv. 31–32, 49–50, 58), paradoxically, like the manna, the physical bread Jesus supplies is said not to be sufficient for sustaining life in its fullness. The gift of manna should have led Israel to 'understand that one does not live by bread alone, but by every word that comes from the mouth of the Lord' (Deuteronomy 8:3). Similarly, the feeding of the 5,000 with food that will perish should have been a sign pointing to the need for being sustained by the revelation of God in Jesus (vv. 26–27). As the true bread from heaven, he will supply those who believe in him with life that is eternal (vv. 40, 47).

Clearly, then, this Gospel has a perspective on a flourishing life that goes beyond everyday existence. The problem is that such existence ends in death and the alienation from the divine life that has produced death impedes human flourishing in a variety of ways. Life is already a divine gift, but to deal with the human predicament, the further gift of eternal life is made available through Jesus. 'Eternal life' and 'life' are largely synonymous in this Gospel. As the life of the age to come, 'eternal' emphasises not simply the unending duration of such life, but the quality that springs from its renewed participation in the divine life. This is human flourishing that is not brought to an end through physical death (vv. 50–51). It begins partially in the present and is not simply about the soul continuing after death, but involves the transformation of the body in a future resurrection (vv. 39–40).

The life-giving revelation in Jesus focuses more specifically on his flesh. It also becomes clear that human enjoyment of a flourishing that overcomes death is obtained through Jesus giving up his own flesh in a violent death (v. 51), and is maintained by continuing to trust in the efficacy of that death. Note the force of the language of eating his flesh and drinking his blood (vv. 53–58).

3 The goal of Jesus' mission

John's Gospel contains a number of mission statements on the lips of Jesus, and this passage has the one that is perhaps most significant for our theme: 'I came that they may have life, and have it abundantly' (v. 10). While this is a relatively well-known saying, the force it receives from its context is often overlooked. It is part of the discourse in which Jesus claims to be both the gate of the sheepfold and the good shepherd. Ezekiel 34, in particular, uses the figure of the shepherd to depict a future time of Israel's flourishing under the rule of God and an ideal Davidic king. Its imagery gives an indication of what would have been expected as part of the abundant life Jesus claims to give as he takes on the dual role of divine shepherd and Davidic servant. The flock will be fed with justice, as corrupt shepherds are rooted out, and the lost, weak and injured are restored (Ezekiel 34:6, 10, 16–22); they will be rescued and liberated from oppressors and enemies (Ezekiel 34:10, 12, 22, 27–28); there will be peace and security (Ezekiel 34:25–28); there will be showers of blessing that ensure feeding on rich pasture and splendid vegetation (Ezekiel 34:14, 26–29); and this flourishing will be accompanied by the sheep's knowledge of their relationship to their shepherd (Ezekiel 34:30–31).

As the gate of the sheepfold (vv. 7, 9), Jesus provides access both to safety within and to abundant pasture without. As the good shepherd (vv. 11–18), he shapes such flourishing distinctively through his own death and resurrection. This Gospel's pervasive post-resurrection perspective allows Jesus to be seen as sovereign over his destiny – laying down his life and taking it up again. He was not simply a victim; his death was noble in that it was voluntary and for the sake of others. Jesus' mission as the good shepherd has as its goal the abundant well-being of the flock, already signified in the abundance of wine at Cana and the abundance of food left over after the feeding of the 5,000. This will be accomplished, paradoxically, through the giving up of his own life, and through the resurrection that completes that act. The abundant life he offers indicates how created life was intended to be, and constitutes a present anticipation of what it will be when fully renewed.

8,000,000

…plastic bags are used in the UK every year. Buy reusable shopping bags instead, preferably made of hard-wearing natural materials, such as hemp.[52]

7,500,000

...tonnes of non-hazardous materials were processed for recycling in 2000 in Canada. From 1998 there was a 60% increase in recycled plastics. The majority of material processed for recycling in 2000 was paper products (39%) and ferrous metals (25%).[53]

6,000,000

– the highest number of hits an eBay auction has ever received, when a wedding dress was auctioned in 2004.[54]

4 Life in the face of death

What can talk of human flourishing mean in the face of death, when even survival is no longer possible? The last sign in Jesus' public mission – the raising of Lazarus – explores more fully this question already touched on in John 6. Here, the significance of the sign is discussed before Jesus actually performs it, and his 'I Am' saying in verse 25 plays a key role. His claim to be both the resurrection and the life underlines that the life he offers takes in the experience of death – through resurrection, a concept that has as its referent human bodily life and not simply a soul or spirit. The next part of Jesus' saying in verses 25–26 spells out what this involves: 'Those who believe in me, even though they die, will live, and everyone who lives and believes in me will never die.'

Its force turns around the different meanings of 'to die' – physical death and spiritual death. Believers in Jesus may undergo physical death, but they will live beyond death because belief in Jesus guarantees resurrection life. In fact, to believe in Jesus is to have that life now and means never experiencing spiritual death, because the quality of the life enjoyed is eternal. Jesus' restoration of Lazarus to ordinary physical life will be a sign pointing beyond itself to this fuller resurrection life. It indicates that, in Christian perspective, flourishing is about created bodily life and has an indispensable future dimension with its hope of resurrection and a renewed creation.

This hope is by no means a denial of death and its consequences that break hearts and shatter families and communities. The depiction of Mary in terms of her weeping at her brother's death, a weeping in which not only the Jewish mourners but Jesus himself participates (vv. 31–35), indicates that grief and lament are entirely appropriate responses to the affront to the divine purposes for full human flourishing that death constitutes.

Martha and, with her, we as readers are asked whether we believe Jesus' claim (v. 26). 'I am the resurrection and the life' would ring hollow if Jesus himself had not overcome death. What underlies this Gospel, and therefore the Lazarus story within it, is the reality of Jesus' own resurrection and the accompanying conviction that, through it, the creator God's 'Yes' to life is louder than death's 'No'.

5 Communal life

In John 13—17, Jesus prepares his followers for their future experience of the abundant life he has offered them. His discourse about the vine and its branches in particular contains themes of importance for their flourishing. With his assertion, 'I am the true vine,' Jesus claims to be the corporate representative of the people of God, fulfilling the role of Israel, the vine that God had planted, and so believers exist as part of the new community centred in him. The main scriptural background for Jesus' discourse is the cluster of passages in Ezekiel 15:1–8, 17:1–10 and 19:10–14, where, as here, there is talk of the vine bearing fruit, a distinction between the vine and its branches, and mention of branches that are good for nothing, that wither and that are thrown into the fire to be burned.

In the new community, God remains the owner of the vineyard, the vine-grower (v. 1) who will either prune and cleanse branches to enable fruit-bearing, or cut away and burn branches that fail to be fruitful. Initial trust in Jesus is not enough. There will be ongoing transformation – pruning – to enable greater flourishing (vv. 2–3, 6). The flourishing of its members comes from a source outside of themselves; they are completely dependent on their relationship to Jesus for any fruitfulness (v. 5). That dependence involves a continuing process whose key requirement is to abide or remain in Jesus (vv. 4–7). In a setting of preparation for his departure, Jesus is able to talk not of his separation from the disciples but of continued connection and union with them.

The flourishing that comes from staying connected to Jesus is characterised by love – both remaining in his love and keeping his commandments to love others (vv. 9–10, 12, 17). It could not be clearer that Jesus' purpose for his followers is their fruit-bearing, and that the primary indication of such fruit is a community that practises love (vv. 16–17). The present experience of abundant eternal life takes the same form as Jesus' costly love, in willingness to lay down our life for another (vv. 12–13). It should not be surprising, given the connotation of the fruit of the vine as the wine of gladness, that the other major characteristic of such flourishing is joy: not simply a temporary happiness but a deep-rooted delight that can still be experienced in the midst of troubles (v. 11).

6 Vocation

John 20:19–23

In contemporary discussions, finding what fulfils you and living it out are considered key factors in spirituality and flourishing, because they give a necessary sense of purpose or vocation. In John, the vocation of Jesus' followers comes as they are caught up in the divine mission of providing life for the world. This is reflected in the crucified and risen Jesus' commissioning of them: 'As the Father has sent me, so I send you' (v. 21). Jesus had been sent both to be the supplier of abundant life and to bear witness to God's purposes for creation (compare 18:37). Now his followers are also to be vehicles of life in the world and to bear communal witness to its intended flourishing. They have already been told their mission is one of witness (15:27). As noted from the vine discourse, this witness to eternal life takes the shape of a community that enacts the pattern of loving service seen in Jesus' life, modelled in the washing of his disciples' feet and epitomised in his willingness to lay down his life for them. The credibility of his followers' missional vocation depends on such embodied witness (13:35).

This vocation needs and receives appropriate resourcing: 'When he had said this, he breathed on them and said, "Receive the Holy Spirit"' (v. 22). In the Jewish scriptures, the Spirit was seen as the source of the future new life of Israel and was characterised in terms of fruitful abundance (e.g. Isaiah 32:15–17; Ezekiel 36:27–30). For John, this Spirit is now linked intimately with Jesus in the inauguration of God's end-time salvation, and has the role of taking from the abundance of life and revelation in Jesus and passing it on to the community (compare 16:15). Just as in the creation account God breathed life into humans (Genesis 2:7), so now Jesus breathes into his followers the new life of the Spirit. The Spirit will be a co-witness (15:26) operating in and through the disciples. Their vocation as witnesses in turn receives its impetus and sustaining power from the Spirit of abundant and flourishing life.

Guidelines

John's Gospel claims that, in a world marred by alienation from the divine life and by death, trust in Jesus' identity and mission, culminating in his death and resurrection, reconnects humans to the triune source of flourishing in the Father, the Son and the Spirit. This reconnection assures us of participation in the fullness of divine life, in an embodied future beyond death.

It is worth reflecting further on possible questions raised by the passages that lie behind that summarised claim.

- Can you relate those experiences in your life in which you feel most fulfilled to any aspects of John's perspective on abundant life?
- How does this Gospel's vision of fruitfulness compare with the values and experiences our society considers necessary for flourishing?
- In what sense, if any, might it be possible to experience flourishing in the midst of adversity or trauma?
- How responsible is talk of abundance and flourishing in a world where scarcity and starvation are the experience of millions? Or could a conviction about God's purposes for an economy of abundance provide a necessary perspective on issues of sustainability?
- What is the relationship between ordinary human life and its flourishing, and the life or eternal life offered by Jesus?

This last question has hovered over all the readings and is related to another question that has occupied Christian thinking about spirituality: what is the relationship between the created human spirit and the divine Spirit within humans? We can propose that the created human spirit is the capacity for self-transcendence within our embodied existence and keeps us open to a transcendent dimension, while the divine Spirit responds to that capacity and its yearning by reaching out in love and reanimating us. Expressing this in a more specifically Christian fashion: the divine Spirit and eternal life take up the spirit and creaturely life already given to humans, but because the latter have become alienated from their source and are in bondage to death, the radical event of Jesus' death and resurrection is required to restore the connection and bring about a transformation in which the divine Spirit and the gift of eternal life make humans more fully alive and enable a flourishing that intensifies, enlarges and perfects their creaturely existence.

FURTHER READING

Brendan Byrne, SJ, *Life Abounding: A reading of John's Gospel* (Liturgical Press, 2014).

Dorothy A. Lee, *Hallowed in Truth and Love: Spirituality in the Johannine literature* (Wipf & Stock, 2012).

Miroslav Volf, *Flourishing: Why we need religion in a globalized world* (Yale University Press, 2015).

Overleaf… Guidelines forthcoming issue | Author profile |
Recommended reading | Order and subscription forms

Guidelines forthcoming issue

DAVID SPRIGGS

A new year always brings to us a sense of new opportunities, even when we know that much of life will actually be much the same. So it is that throughout this coming year our lectionary Gospel will be Luke, which for most of us will be material we have read many times and, indeed, covered in *Guidelines* many times. But we will be guided through the second half of this endearing Gospel by Dr Steve Walton, and so will have the opportunity to see it with fresh eyes and discover new and significant things about Jesus the Saviour, as well as receive fresh challenges about our own leadership and mission.

On this biblical bedrock the rest of these notes will be built. 'Leadership for kingdom building' is one such contribution. Martin Lee has recently retired as CEO for Global Connections. He will utilise his knowledge of the church worldwide as well as his own experience of leading Christian organisations to share with us the challenges, pitfalls and opportunities for those who are called to be leaders in the Christian community.

The Gospel of Luke announces the birth of Jesus as an outpouring of peace on earth. Among new writers for this issue of *Guidelines* is Andrew Francis. He will focus on this topic through his notes on 'Shalom', bringing to us through the text his insights gleaned from many years involved in mediation processes.

Mentioning gleaning brings us to Pauline Hoggarth, another new writer. Her contribution is on the delightful story of the book of Ruth. By the time we get to the gleaning in this story, it is becoming delightful, but it is also strangely relevant today, for essentially the plotline is about migration, death, poverty and vulnerability. Within and beyond this, there is the action of God, who rescues even in these terrifying circumstances.

Naomi and Ruth remind us that God has always chosen women as well as men in his redemptive story. Jill Duff's helpful reflections on other women, especially those we meet in Luke's Gospel, will complement this focus.

While this issue begins with the new year, it leads on rapidly to Lent and the Passion. Here, two familiar authors write for us. Alec Gilmore invites us to take a fresh approach to Lent through his contribution on 'Lenten laughter'. Ian Paul takes on the baton as he looks backwards from the perspective of Acts on the Passion and resurrection. This serves to remind us that all the New Testament is a post-Easter document and these central acts of our redemption have impact and implications for the Christian church throughout all time.

In addition to this wealth of contributions, we also have Dr Andrew Mayes encouraging us to use the Bible to deepen our spirituality. He opens our eyes (or perhaps it would be more appropriate to say 'our five senses') to the intense physicality of the fourth Gospel as a means of appreciating the reality of the incarnation. At the same time, he brings deep challenges to us to develop our own spirituality.

Finally, I mention Fr Henry Wansbrough exploring 1 Chronicles, and Torsten Uhlig, another new author, who focuses on some core themes in Isaiah.

Author profile: Paul Bradbury

First and foremost, the Bible matters to me because it is an absolutely fundamental part of the staple diet for sustaining my discipleship of Jesus. I don't think that the close relationship in the Bible between the written word of God and food is simply a metaphor. 'Eat this scroll,' says God to Ezekiel (Ezekiel 3:1) as he is called to speak the words of God to the house of Israel. Likewise, Jesus compares God's words to the life-giving sustenance of bread (Matthew 4:4).

The Bible is real food. Food for the soul. I read the Bible in order for these words to become part of me. To a very great extent, we are what we eat (or consume), in which case I am committed to consuming the Bible as the basis for my life. It is hard, therefore, to always be specific about the particular ways in which the Bible has informed decisions or opinions – but day after day, week after week, year after year, daily reading of the Bible has formed me and is forming me still.

I believe that the key testimony of its power in my life is the way in which the stories of the Bible have shaped my own. While the Bible is certainly a library, with a host of different genres represented, it nevertheless presents a narrative: a grand narrative of the history of creation, one in which we have an important role to play. This fundamentally shapes how we choose to live as a family: the solar panels on the roof of our house; the rhythm of our week and year; the vocations we are seeking to follow; the attitude we try to have towards our neighbours. And within this grand narrative are smaller vignettes which throw beams of light on particular areas of life, often at the most opportune times.

I remember in particular when we had a tough time as a newly married couple, following the birth of our first child. He was ill for some months before being diagnosed with a chronic lung condition, which he still lives with today. We went on holiday to recover from this experience and, while we were away, our flat in London was flooded. We lost almost everything. At that time, I discovered first of all the book of Job and secondly psalms of lament. Neither of those elements of the big story of the Bible gave me answers to the questions, doubt and confusion we suffered at the time. But there in the Bible was the language of protest, pain and praise in the context of suffering. I am not sure I would have made it without the book of Job. That story vindicated my experience and said it was okay to doubt, to rage, to question God's promises and God's character and still be a Christian.

An extract from
Is Your God Too Small?

'Where can wisdom be found?' (Job 24:12)

Is Your God Too Small? faces that question head-on. Job struggled with huge questions about suffering – his own and the world's. He looked for an answer in the past, but discovered that it lay elsewhere, in God and in the divine presence. This accessible book opens Job for today's church, encouraging us to enlarge our view of God and his goodness in difficult times, making it a must-read in the context of the world's problems today.

If Job's struggle teaches us anything, it teaches us that God is not 'nice'. There is a bigness about God that dwarfs us – dwarfs our virtue, our understanding, our theology. We do not have enough words in our vocabulary to describe him. His holiness is beyond our purest thoughts, his knowledge more comprehensive than the most encyclopedic libraries can embrace, his wisdom beyond what the most profound philosophy can begin to deduce, his eternity simply unimaginable to time-bound thought…

Not surprisingly, many who turn to the book of Job do so hoping to find an answer to the problem of suffering. Surely here, in the story of one man's legendary experience of unrelenting pain, we can find a way of responding to that lifelong question: Why? So what can we say with certainty?

First, there are no easy answers! For Job's friends, there was one obvious explanation that, had Job been more honest with himself (in their view), he would have accepted. They were wrong. The reason for Job's suffering remained out of reach to them and to Job. They would never have come close to finding it even if they had debated for years.

Second, suffering cannot be explained as simply as drawing a straight line between sin and punishment. Granted, the Bible does make that link from time to time, both generally and in specific instances. Clearly the world would be a different place if sin had not entered. We see that in the consequences of Adam and Eve's sin (Genesis 3:14–19), and in the enormous contrast with the new heaven and earth (Revelation 21:1–8). God warned his people that disobedience would give physical and natural consequences like famine and exile (e.g. Deuteronomy 28). Paul mentions that some Christians in Corinth were ill because they had abused the Lord's Supper (1 Corinthians 11:30), and James hints at the possibility of a link between sin and sickness in some cases (James 5:15). But to argue, as Job's friends did, that sickness is invariably punishment for sin is a serious mistake.

Third, Satan – or 'the Satan' as the book of Job describes the devil, intending to focus attention on his role as an adversary rather than his personhood – is limited in his power. He may accuse but is not at liberty to harm God's children except the Father permits it. We do not need to fear him if we remain close to God. In his classic tale, *Pilgrim's Progress*, John Bunyan imagines the devil as a lion on Christian's path, but he is chained! At the same time, we would be foolish to dismiss him as a figure of fun dressed in a red leotard carrying a three-pronged fork.

Fourth, if the book of Job has anything to teach us about suffering, it is not so much an explanation we need, but an experience of God himself, to learn the fear of God that gives wisdom. Disturbing that may be, but nothing will be more fulfilling, more likely to bring us peace. This was certainly the case for Job and can be for us, which is why I suggested that the book of Job is more about God than the human experience of tragedy and pain. What we learn from God here may seriously challenge what we have always believed about him.

To order a copy of this book, please use the order form on page 151.

Recommended reading

Few would doubt that we live in a wounded and broken world. But God has sent a Saviour, Jesus Christ, who calls us, in the beatitudes, to live an authentic, countercultural lifestyle. By being different we can make a difference, becoming the salt of the earth and the light of the world.

Living Differently to Make a Difference
The beatitudes and countercultural lifestyle
Will Donaldson
978 0 85746 671 6 £7.99
brfonline.org.uk

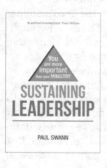

Through telling his story of brokenness and fragility through to healing and restoration, Paul Swann offers an insight into that journey and draws from it lessons for not only surviving but thriving in ministry.

Sustaining Leadership
You are more important than your ministry
Paul Swann
978 0 85746 651 8 £7.99
brfonline.org.uk

Reflecting on the Jonah story, this book finds powerful connections between the call and mission of Jonah and the mission context of our own time. It argues for a ministry rooted in grace, where God shapes who we are.

Stepping into Grace
Moving beyond ambition to contemplative mission
Paul Bradbury
978 0 85746 523 8 £7.99
brfonline.org.uk

To order

Online: brfonline.org.uk
Telephone: +44 (0)1865 319700
Mon–Fri 9.15–17.30

Delivery times within the UK are normally
15 working days. Prices are correct at the time of
going to press but may change without prior notice.

Title	Price	Qty	Total
Is Your God Too Small?	£7.99		
Living Differently to Make a Difference	£7.99		
Sustaining Leadership	£7.99		
Stepping into Grace	£7.99		

POSTAGE AND PACKING CHARGES			
Order value	UK	Europe	Rest of world
Under £7.00	£2.00	£5.00	£7.00
£7.00–£29.99	£3.00	£9.00	£15.00
£30.00 and over	FREE	£9.00 + 15% of order value	£15.00 + 20% of order value

Total value of books	
Postage and packing	
Total for this order	

Please complete in BLOCK CAPITALS

Title _____ First name/initials _____ Surname _____

Address _____

_____ Postcode _____

Acc. No. _____ Telephone _____

Email _____

Method of payment

☐ Cheque (made payable to BRF) ☐ MasterCard / Visa

Card no. ☐☐☐☐ ☐☐☐☐ ☐☐☐☐ ☐☐☐☐

Valid from ☐☐ ☐☐ Expires ☐☐ ☐☐ Security code* ☐☐☐

Last 3 digits on the reverse of the card

Signature* _____ Date _____ / _____ / _____

*ESSENTIAL IN ORDER TO PROCESS YOUR ORDER

Please return this form to: BRF, 15 The Chambers, Vineyard, Abingdon OX14 3FE | enquiries@brf.org.uk
To read our terms and find out about cancelling your order, please visit **brfonline.org.uk/terms**.

The Bible Reading Fellowship (BRF) is a Registered Charity (233280)

Make a lasting difference through a gift in your will

Across England, and in many parts of the world, children are beginning school after the summer holidays. Some will start studying new subjects this year or will be preparing for important exams; others will be going to school for the very first time with equal levels of excitement and trepidation.

Our school years are an important time of growth and preparation. We learn all sorts of things, from the square root of 56 to the start of World War II (in case you're wondering, the answers are 7.48 and 1 September 1939). Yet it's often the soft skills we develop that we continue to draw on throughout our lives: things such as how to work effectively with other people or how to deal with conflict and disappointment.

At BRF, we're passionate about transforming lives and communities through the Christian faith. One of the ways we do this is by teaching about Christian values and the Bible in schools through Barnabas RE Days. These explore values such as friendship, community and resilience; and ask questions like 'What is character?' and 'How does it form the people that we are and the communities we belong to?'

Around 23,200 children experienced our Barnabas RE Days and related events last year, and over 25,500 ideas for classroom studies and assemblies were downloaded from our website. Much of this work is only possible because of the generosity of those who support us during their lifetime and through gifts in wills.

Gifts in wills are an important source of income for us and they don't need to be huge to make a real difference. Will you help us transform more lives and communities through a gift in your will?

For further information about making a gift to BRF in your will, please visit **brf.org.uk/lastingdifference**, contact Sophie Aldred on **+44 (0)1865 319700** or email **giving@brf.org.uk**.

Whatever you can do or give, we thank you for your support.

SHARING OUR VISION – MAKING A GIFT

I would like to make a gift to support BRF. Please use my gift for:

☐ where it is needed most ☐ Barnabas in Schools ☐ Parenting for Faith
☐ Messy Church ☐ Who Let The Dads Out? ☐ The Gift of Years

Title	First name/initials	Surname

Address

	Postcode

Email

Telephone

Signature	Date

giftaid it You can add an extra 25p to every £1 you give.

Please treat as Gift Aid donations all qualifying gifts of money made

☐ today, ☐ in the past four years, ☐ and in the future.

I am a UK taxpayer and understand that if I pay less Income Tax and/or Capital Gains Tax in the current tax year than the amount of Gift Aid claimed on all my donations, it is my responsibility to pay any difference.

☐ My donation does not qualify for Gift Aid.

Please notify BRF if you want to cancel this Gift Aid declaration, change your name or home address, or no longer pay sufficient tax on your income and/or capital gains.

Please complete other side of form ➜

Please return this form to:
BRF, 15 The Chambers, Vineyard, Abingdon OX14 3FE

The Bible Reading Fellowship is a Registered Charity (233280)

SHARING OUR VISION – MAKING A GIFT

Regular giving

By Direct Debit:

☐ I would like to make a regular gift of £ [   ] per month/quarter/year.
Please also complete the Direct Debit instruction on page 159.

By Standing Order:

Please contact Priscilla Kew +44 (0)1235 462305 | giving@brf.org.uk

One-off donation

Please accept my gift of:

☐ £10 ☐ £50 ☐ £100 Other £ [   ]

by (delete as appropriate):

☐ Cheque/Charity Voucher payable to 'BRF'

☐ MasterCard/Visa/Debit card/Charity card

Name on card [   ]

Card no. [   ] [   ] [   ] [   ]

Valid from [M M Y Y] Expires [M M Y Y]

Security code* [   ] *Last 3 digits on the reverse of the card
ESSENTIAL IN ORDER TO PROCESS YOUR PAYMENT

Signature [   ] Date [   ]

We like to acknowledge all donations. However, if you do not wish to receive an acknowledgement, please tick here ☐

☜ Please complete other side of form

Please return this form to:
BRF, 15 The Chambers, Vineyard, Abingdon OX14 3FE

BRF

The Bible Reading Fellowship is a Registered Charity (233280)

GL0318

GUIDELINES SUBSCRIPTION RATES

Please note our new subscription rates, current until 30 April 2019:

Individual subscriptions
covering 3 issues for under 5 copies, payable in advance
(including postage & packing):

	UK	Europe	Rest of world
Guidelines 1-year subscription	£16.95	£25.20	£29.10
Guidelines 3-year subscription (9 issues)	£46.35	N/A	N/A

Group subscriptions
covering 3 issues for 5 copies or more, sent to **one** UK address (post free):

Guidelines 1-year subscription	£13.50 per set of 3 issues p.a.

Please note that the annual billing period for group subscriptions runs from
1 May to 30 April.

Overseas group subscription rates
Available on request. Please email **enquiries@brf.org.uk**.

Copies may also be obtained from Christian bookshops:

Guidelines	£4.50 per copy

All our Bible reading notes can be ordered online by visiting
biblereadingnotes.org.uk/subscriptions

For information about our other Bible reading notes,
and apps for iPhone and iPod touch, visit
biblereadingnotes.org.uk

All our Bible reading notes can be ordered online by visiting
biblereadingnotes.org.uk/subscriptions

☐ I would like to take out a subscription:

Title _____ First name/initials _____ Surname _____

Address _____

_____ Postcode _____

Telephone _____ Email _____

Please send *Guidelines* beginning with the January 2019 / May 2019 / September 2019
issue (*delete as appropriate*):

(please tick box)

		UK	Europe	Rest of world
Guidelines 1-year subscription		☐ £16.95	☐ £25.20	☐ £29.10
Guidelines 3-year subscription		☐ £46.35	N/A	N/A

Total enclosed £ _____ (cheques should be made payable to 'BRF')

Please charge my MasterCard / Visa ☐ Debit card ☐ with £ _____

Card no. ☐☐☐☐ ☐☐☐☐ ☐☐☐☐ ☐☐☐☐

Valid from ☐☐/☐☐ Expires ☐☐/☐☐ Security code* ☐☐☐

<small>Last 3 digits on the reverse of the card</small>

Signature* _____ Date _____/_____/_____

*ESSENTIAL IN ORDER TO PROCESS YOUR PAYMENT

To set up a Direct Debit, please also complete the Direct Debit instruction on page 159 and
return it to BRF with this form.

Please return this form with the appropriate payment to:
BRF, 15 The Chambers, Vineyard, Abingdon OX14 3FE

To read our terms and find out about cancelling your order, please visit **brfonline.org.uk/terms**.

The Bible Reading Fellowship (BRF) is a Registered Charity (233280)

GUIDELINES GIFT SUBSCRIPTION FORM

☐ I would like to give a gift subscription (please provide both names and addresses):

Title .... First name/initials .... Surname ....

Address ....

.... Postcode ....

Telephone .... Email ....

Gift subscription name ....

Gift subscription address ....

.... Postcode ....

Gift message (20 words max. or include your own gift card):

....

....

Please send *Guidelines* beginning with the January 2019 / May 2019 / September 2019 issue (*delete as appropriate*):

(please tick box)	UK	Europe	Rest of world
Guidelines 1-year subscription	☐ £16.95	☐ £25.20	☐ £29.10
Guidelines 3-year subscription	☐ £46.35	N/A	N/A

Total enclosed £ .... (cheques should be made payable to 'BRF')

Please charge my MasterCard / Visa ☐ Debit card ☐ with £ ....

Card no. ☐☐☐☐ ☐☐☐☐ ☐☐☐☐ ☐☐☐☐

Valid from ☐☐ ☐☐ Expires ☐☐ ☐☐ Security code* ☐☐☐

Last 3 digits on the reverse of the card

Signature* .... Date ....../....../......

*ESSENTIAL IN ORDER TO PROCESS YOUR PAYMENT

To set up a Direct Debit, please also complete the Direct Debit instruction on page 159 and return it to BRF with this form.

Please return this form with the appropriate payment to:
BRF, 15 The Chambers, Vineyard, Abingdon OX14 3FE

To read our terms and find out about cancelling your order, please visit **brfonline.org.uk/terms**.

You can pay for your annual subscription to our Bible reading notes using Direct Debit. You need only give your bank details once, and the payment is made automatically every year until you cancel it. If you would like to pay by Direct Debit, please use the form opposite, entering your BRF account number under 'Reference number'.

You are fully covered by the Direct Debit Guarantee:

The Direct Debit Guarantee

- This Guarantee is offered by all banks and building societies that accept instructions to pay Direct Debits.

- If there are any changes to the amount, date or frequency of your Direct Debit, The Bible Reading Fellowship will notify you 10 working days in advance of your account being debited or as otherwise agreed. If you request The Bible Reading Fellowship to collect a payment, confirmation of the amount and date will be given to you at the time of the request.

- If an error is made in the payment of your Direct Debit, by The Bible Reading Fellowship or your bank or building society, you are entitled to a full and immediate refund of the amount paid from your bank or building society.

- If you receive a refund you are not entitled to, you must pay it back when The Bible Reading Fellowship asks you to.

- You can cancel a Direct Debit at any time by simply contacting your bank or building society. Written confirmation may be required. Please also notify us.

GL0318

The Bible Reading Fellowship

Instruction to your bank or building society to pay by Direct Debit

Please fill in the whole form using a ballpoint pen and return it to:
BRF, 15 The Chambers, Vineyard, Abingdon OX14 3FE

Service User Number:

5	5	8	2	2	9

Name and full postal address of your bank or building society

To: The Manager	Bank/Building Society
Address	
	Postcode

Name(s) of account holder(s)

Branch sort code

☐☐ - ☐☐ - ☐☐

Bank/Building Society account number

☐☐☐☐☐☐☐☐

Reference number

☐☐☐☐☐☐☐☐

Instruction to your Bank/Building Society

Please pay The Bible Reading Fellowship Direct Debits from the account detailed
in this instruction, subject to the safeguards assured by the Direct Debit Guarantee.
I understand that this instruction may remain with The Bible Reading Fellowship and, if so,
details will be passed electronically to my bank/building society.

Signature(s)

Banks and Building Societies may not accept Direct Debit instructions for some types
of account.

Transforming
lives and communities

Christian growth and understanding of the Bible

Resourcing individuals, groups and leaders in churches for their own
spiritual journey and for their ministry

Church outreach in the local community

Offering three programmes that churches are embracing
to great effect as they seek to engage
with their local communities
and transform lives

Teaching Christianity in primary schools

Working with children and teachers to explore Christianity creatively
and confidently

Children's and family ministry

Working with churches and families to explore Christianity creatively
and bring the Bible alive

Visit **brf.org.uk** for more information on BRF's work

brf.org.uk